EMERGING FROM

DARKNESS INTO LIGHT

ZUANÍA MOLINA

Emerging from Darkness into Light © 2021 Zuanía Molina
ISBN: 9798843142650
Independent Publishing
Editors: Wilma Ortiz
Chanía & Zachary Wright (English version)
Amneris Meléndez (Spanish version)
Translation: Chanía Wright
Cover: Wigberto Santiago @Diseno, Inc.
Photography: Bethany Carpio
For invitations or orders:
zuaniamolina@yahoo.com

DEDICATION

First and foremost, I want to dedicate this book to my beloved God. I give it as my most precious first fruit. God, I want to dedicate this book to you for all you have done in my life and to show you my endless gratitude. The best thing that has ever happened to me is being able to meet and serve you. My longing is for you to always be my greatest inspiration.

Secondly, I want to dedicate this book to my best friend and life-long partner, my beloved husband Rafael Oropeza, better known as Chapi. Our love story has been a beautiful one, even with all the difficult moments we have faced. These moments have allowed us to grow and mature together, but above all they have made us understand the true meaning of love. "He who can love can handle everything." Thank you for being the number one accomplice in all my adventures. Thank you for always being you. Thank you for being my inspiration. I love you!

To my firstborn Chanía, "Mi canelita de Mamá," which is how I like to call her. This translates to "Mama's little cinnamon." Daughter of my life, you know I have always told you that you came into our lives to change them for the better. You are our greatest blessing. I thank God for the daughter you have been - a beautiful, loving, helpful and hardworking daughter. I am super proud of you. Thank you for loving me as you do and for always being next to me. Thank you for being my inspiration. Your life changed our stories. I love you!

To my boy, my beloved son Adriel. Son, you were our answered prayer. You are the prince and the model (you have always cared most about your appearance) of our house. Your spontaneity and your personality have always kept us active. You are more than what we dreamed of. Thank you for your unconditional support, for being my number one fan, and for being the first to ask me for a copy of my book. Your dad and I are immensely proud of the man you have become. Thank you for being my inspiration. I love you!

Lastly, I would like to dedicate this book to our beloved daughter, our forever baby, Guainía Ananí. You are my beautiful water flower. My love, from the moment I knew you were in my womb, I knew you were special. God has taught us so much through you. For this and many other reasons, we will always be grateful for you. As a person you carry so much love for everyone. You are sensitive, simple, humble, and genuine. Your character models the character of Christ, and that my daughter, says a lot about who you are. My beautiful girl, thanks for completing our lives. Thank you for being my inspiration. I love you!

INTRODUCTION

This book, in a brief way, tells the story of me and my husband's life, from the first day we met. Throughout this book I will be sharing anecdotes and experiences that have changed our lives.

One reason I have decided to share our stories with you is so that you can relate to them. The main reason I am sharing these stories is so that you can get to know the God who transformed our lives in a supernatural way.

This book aims to help you understand, in a simple and straightforward way, the importance of making correct decisions from adolescence to adulthood. Here you will read some stories from my life that reflect real-life problems and how having a relationship with God, the Father, makes a big difference in making decisions. In this book I will talk about topics such as teen pregnancy, pornography, and infidelity, among others.

We all go through moments in life where we are confronted by our weaknesses, but it is up to us to be wise and know how to choose what we need and not what we want.

This book's target audience is both men and women, regardless of their age. Here you will find a series of reflections that will motivate you to know a God of love.

I am a woman who loves God and her family above all things. A woman who loves nature, the arts, and writing. That is why, through this writing, I want to be able to express who I am, in a simple and genuine way. I pray to the Father, the Son, and the Holy Spirit that every chapter will be of impact and transformation to your life.

Each of these chapters are inspired by the Holy Spirit for you. As I wrote them, I prayed for you so that, like me, you can also experience transformation. Sit back and enjoy this time where you, the Holy Spirit, and I will be together.

See you in the next chapter,

Zuania Molina

Table of Content

CHAPTER 1

As a Young Girl I Met the Love of My Life

My husband and I met in the summer of 1993. I was thirteen and Chapi was seventeen. I remember that day as if it were today. I was in my room watching television when my older sister, Adriana, came into my room out of nowhere and asked if I wanted to go to Old San Juan (an exceptionally beautiful and historic area in the capital of Puerto Rico) to hang out with her. I, surprised by this invitation, (since she did not tend to invite me to go out with her) asked her, "Why are you inviting me?" She confessed that they were going with some friends and that Abraham was taking his youngest brother. Since everyone was going in couples, she did not want him to be alone. My first thought was that I did want to go because I would have the opportunity to spend time with my sister and her friends, but mostly because it will give me the opportunity to see what she did with her friends. I used to want to be like her in many ways, so I could not miss an opportunity like this that would help me perfect the ability to emulate her. So, to disguise the desperate desire of me wanting to go, I asked her what Abraham's brother was like, specifically, if he looked like him. My brother-in-law has always been handsome. I wanted to make sure that his younger brother would not disappoint me - remember, I was thirteen and at that age, we are very selective and demanding when it comes to physical appearance. However, I know many women, who still at my age, still think this way.

In short, Adriana told me that Chapi (which is his childhood nickname) only looked a little bit like him but was "chubbier" than Abraham. When she told me that, I automatically replied to her with a frustrated tone, "That means he looks like a cow!" To this day, I do not understand why I said that because my brother-in-law was extremely skinny. Adri, how I call her out of love, answered me, "Girl no! He is a 'surfer' too. What I meant is that he is a little bulkier than Abraham and darker." That part caught my attention because I had always liked boys with darker skin and those that lived a beach lifestyle.

During that time, my style was more "rapper." In those days, there were these super "high waisted" skinny jeans of a brand called Parasuco that I used to wear with my black high-top Converse. My hairstyle was a high ponytail, either with the hair completely put up or the half up half down. This look was expertly achieved with the Volumax hair gel that gave me the slick look or "Lambía de vaca," like we call it in Puerto Rico that translates to "Cow lick." The higher the ponytail, the more "in" (fashionable) you were. Oh! And I cannot forget about the hoop earrings; the bigger the better. The last touch was the dark brown lipstick or burgundy, which needed to be very intense… Ha, ha, ha. My God, I hope you understand all these terms. Anyways, that was my nineties style.

The problem was that my style did not match with theirs. At that time, my sister and her group were the biggest fans of the music genres Techno, Rock, and Alternative, and more styles that I liked but were not of my preferences. Her style was… How can I explain it? They were very "free" in the sense of how they dressed! Ha, ha, ha… This meant that my style would not fit with theirs.

So, my sister told me that she was going to give me a makeover and that was the only way or condition for me to go with them. She let me borrow her orange palazzo pants that had a very colorful boho print. She combined it with her cream crop top that had a baggie fit on me, but that was the surfer style she was going for with me. I remember that when I looked at myself in the mirror my first words were, "Girl! What have you done? I look like a clown." She ignored my comment because she was sure of her masterpiece and replied to me, "Well stay dressed as a clown, because that's how you are going."

Even though I was scared, I did not change my clothes because I trusted her good taste. My sister has always had a good eye for fashion. She has always been very original and a pioneer with everything she invents or designs. Because of that, I always wanted to copy her but when I tried it, it never fit me as well as it did her. Only Adriana can wear the peculiar combinations that she comes up with. Okay, let us continue with the story. Where did we leave off? Oh yes…When she told me to stay dressed as a clown. Well, I fixed myself up and went to the living room to wait for my sister to finish getting ready. Out of nowhere, I saw a green truck in front of my house and then I heard a honk. Adriana shouted for me to go outside because that was Abraham's brother that came to pick us up to take us to their home where everyone planned on meeting. When she shouted to me from her room (since she was not ready), I felt as if my body got as cold as ice. I got up from the chair and went to her room. I opened the door and told her, "Girl, how embarrassing. I am not going outside without you!" She replied, "Zuanía, don't be so lame and go and tell him to wait a minute and that I still haven't finished getting dressed."

I do not know where I got the strength from, but I went. When I walked towards the car and I finally saw him, I am not going to lie, my stomach was full of butterflies. At that moment, I was able to experience love at first sight. It was like cupid hit me with his bow and arrow. Oh God, I think I heard birds singing and even a light came out of him… Ha, ha, ha, ha. It sounds exaggerated, but I really felt the butterflies. I fell in love at that first moment I saw him. He met all the requirements that this thirteen-year-old girl demanded on her list of the ideal physique.

I managed to get close to him as he was leaning back on the door of the car with his hands crossed. I remember as if it were yesterday. He was wearing an orange polo shirt, a pair of light blue jeans, a pair of Reef sandals, which was the brand that the surfers tend to use, and some multicolored glasses that were also in style at that time. He looked perfect, his style went accordingly with his physique and his skin, perfectly tan. My God that skin color drove me crazy! It was that tan dark-skinned color that you know you can only get from the beach. As I walked towards him, he smiled, and I felt my legs automatically get weak. That smile, to this day, is the one that melts me, even in the moments when we disagree or have faced different conflicts. I will forever be in love with his smile.

When I got near him, he said to me, "Hello, how are you? You must be Zuanía. My name is Rafael, but they call me Chapi. It is a pleasure to meet you," while he reached out his hand to greet me. Well, imagine a choir of angels singing because that is what I heard that day. His voice was perfect; it was in harmony with his body. I tried to hide my emotions as much as I could and answered "Hello, it is a pleasure." Then I followed with the message my sister had sent me to say. Today, he tells me that he noticed my nervousness and the embarrassment I felt while I talked to him. He says that was something that he liked and thought it was adorable. When I finished giving him the message, I told him, "Well, when she's done, we'll leave, okay?" I turned around and while I walked to the house he told me, "I like your pants." When I heard him, it felt as if someone was pouring a bucket of ice-cold water over me; I was completely frozen. The only thing that I was able to reply was, "Thanks." Without turning around to look at him, I started walking faster towards the house. When I got inside, I went to Adri. She noticed my face and started laughing and told me, "See, I told you he was also cute, but Abraham is cuter." I did not say anything due to me being so embarrassed. The only thing I could do was laugh and tell her, "How embarrassing!"

When we arrived at Old San Juan, I remember we walked almost every street. While we walked, the only thing I did was listen to them talk. I felt so much embarrassment for being close to Chapi. I did not even have the guts to talk to him. He every now and then would look at me and ask, "You're not going to talk?" while he laughed, because he knew I was nervous. I could not even reply, the only thing I could do is just laugh.

Later that night we went to the house of one of Adri's friends to listen to some music and look at different CD covers. While they listened to music, Chapi and I were sitting on a green sofa. The sofa was very fluffy and soft; so fluffy that we sank in as we sat down. He was the one that started talking to me. He asked me so many questions, from what was my favorite type of music to if I had a boyfriend, which I rapidly replied with, "No, I do not have a boyfriend. How about you? Do you have a girlfriend?" Even I got surprised at how fast that question came out of my mouth. He was laughing, but at the same time, was embarrassed because of what he was about to say. "Yes, I have a girlfriend and we have been together for 4 years." I cannot remember which emotion I felt first…anger, deception, sadness, or the urge to laugh. The point was that since he told me that, I got on guard and the way I was talking to him completely changed. "You have a girlfriend and you're here with me?" He started behaving like a "saint," trying to justify his actions with me. He replied, "But I am not doing anything bad. We are just talking," while he smiled in a mocking manner because he knew he was lying. Just like me, he knew very well that we spent all that afternoon flirting. The chemistry that we both felt from that first moment, we saw each other as being compatible and what we felt was inexplicable.

The problem was that he was in a relationship, one of which he had been in for years. His girlfriend was his first girlfriend. They had been together since they were thirteen and he had met her in his neighborhood. He lived two streets in front of hers. Now we found ourselves in an uncomfortable situation, but at the same time exciting. What we were feeling for one another was real and we did not know how to handle it.

I can imagine what you could be thinking... "What a dummy!" That should have been the moment where I stopped everything and cut any feelings that had grown. You are right, I should have done that, but I did not. I continued with the game of words, and we became more involved with one another. Bravely, at the end of the night he had the nerve to ask for my phone number and I gave it to him.

It was not until two weeks later that he called. When I received the call, the first thing I asked Chapi was why did not he call me sooner. His excuse was that he did not have the guts, but later I found out that the real reason he was calling was because he was going through one of his usual breakups with his girlfriend. That is how our relationship started; me being the "Other woman."

FRIENDS OR PARENTS TO OUR CHILDREN

Today I look back and I see the way we managed the situation. Even though I laugh for how ignorant we both were, I can see many factors that make me thank God for the simple fact that I was able to know Him. To see how we kept flirting with each other knowing that he was already in a relationship was obviously very shameful, especially at my youthful age.

Now that I am a mother, I cannot even imagine that one of my children would go through the same thing we lived through. Even though I am open-minded about talking about these issues with them, I would never agree that they should behave the way we both did. While the illusion of love is inevitable at these ages and very valid, I also recognize the significant role that we as parents play in helping them redirect their thoughts and actions towards a healthier way of thinking, making the right decisions at every stage of our life. I have heard so many people say, "My kids and I are best friends" or "I am not just their parent, I am their best friend." Although sometimes the intention in which how this is communicated is not bad, the simple action brings consequences that are not beneficial to the parent nor child. Our children do not need to see us as one of their peers. They need a paternal figure to guide them and help them become a person who brings their best to society. Becoming friends does not give us more confidence or more freedom in our relationship, just like being a parent does not limit us from having one. Relationships between parents and children should be fostered in love, trust, tolerance, patience, and effective communication, but most importantly love.

"For now, we see only a reflection as in a mirror; then we shall see face to face. Now I know in part; then I shall know fully, even as I am fully known. And now these three remain: faith, hope and love. But the greatest of these is love."
(1 Corinthians 13:12-13 NIV)

The Bible teaches us that love covers multitudes of sins.

"Above all, love each other deeply, because love covers over a multitude of sins."
(1 Peter 4:8 NIV)

A relationship based on love, especially when we understand the meaning through the eyes of God, always gives us the security and peace when making the right decisions for the benefit of others and ourselves. Teaching and modeling are the foundations of being parents; that is the essence of our role from the moment our children are born. A relationship where our children view us as a friend can bring confusion for both the child and the parent, as roles often can be reversed and misused. For example, wanting to be our kid's friend and feeling that we can tell them all our problems, that as adults we face, can create a bad picture of who we are and model a bad version of ourselves on how they should behave in a comparable situation. In these cases, adults should look for mature and experienced people with whom we can vent and who can help us understand what is right so that we can set an example to our children. I understand that every situation is different and that sometimes the family nucleus is not the same in every home. Perhaps, you are a single parent, grandparent, aunt or uncle, or maybe you're a mentor to someone; it doesn't matter. The foundation remains the same, teaching and modeling. A child or young adult, no matter how intelligent, does not have the same mental capacity as an adult. That is the law of nature. That is why the external influence of every developmental stage of a human life is so important.

When I tell our story to our children, I emphasize the importance of living lives that please God. I give them a comparison of how it is to live a life outside of Him and how beautiful it is to do His will, even though it comes with many sacrifices. I taught them that the story their parents lived is another example that shows the condition in which the world has always lived. A system where values and doing the right thing become second place and your own feelings become first. The desire to satisfy your wants and needs no matter the consequences, whether it goes against what is right, or if it will hurt someone else or yourself. Because the important thing is to live in the moment and satisfy a momentary pleasure that will only fill that moment. These are the things that happen when a life does not have Christ in it. This becomes "The daily bread" for all those who live a life disconnected from God, who shows us what is true, real, and right... a life with God is a life with purpose and meaning. *"'For I know the plans I have for you,' declares the LORD, "plans to prosper you and not to harm you, plans to give you hope and a future.'"(Jeremiah 29:11 NIV)*

CHAPTER 2

So Young and I Was Already the Other Girl

I remember that I used to like to make Chapi nervous by going to the places where I knew he was going to be with his girlfriend. One day I was at the movie theater with a couple of my friends, and I found out that he was also there with her, so I automatically went to where they were. By that time, I was 14 years old, and I remember they were in the arcade area. When I entered the arcade, he became super nervous, but knew how to disguise it very well. I, very daringly, headed toward him. The closer I got, the more his eyes got wider. I did not do anything, just walked over to his side, and rubbed his hand on mine. No one noticed because the place was full of people.

We played this game for several months until one day, I told him that I was tired of being the other girl and that he had to decide who he wanted to be with. Unbelievably, I felt super bad for what I did; there was a voice inside of me telling me to stop. I know this made him feel bad too. However, he was honest from the first day we met. I was also responsible for this because I knew that he

17

had a girlfriend, but I continued to play games and act in ways I should not have acted. He always told me that he felt bad for his actions with me, but both of us were tied to a life of sin and it made it difficult to get away from this guilty pleasure, even if it was not right. I do not quite remember how it went exactly, but I know that in one of our arguments, I told him that I had made the decision to stop and so I did.

We did not talk for a couple of months. I only knew about him because of the little I heard when my sister and my brother-in-law mentioned him in their conversations. Every time I heard his name, everything within me shuddered, but I managed to be strong and not fall into the temptation to call him.

One day, Adriana came to me and said, "I think Chapi left his girlfriend for good." I remember that my automatic answer was, "He is always leaving her. I do not see what the difference is now." She replied that they had not been talking and had not seen each other for several months; that the girl and her family had moved out of the neighborhood. She also told me that sometimes he asked about me. My heart started beating super-fast, but I still contained the desire of wanting to call him and I answered her, "Good for him."

WHEN A BAD HABIT BECOMES A CUSTOM

You might think, "Well, you were too young to understand what was right." To an extent, you are right, but age does not justify a bad action especially when done with consciousness. A bad action that is not corrected in time can turn into a bad habit.

Everyone, no matter whether you are a believer or not, has heard that voice within us that says, "Stop, don't do it." You can call it as you like, your subconscious, the good side, the divinity, the universe, or an angel. In my case, I am clear that it is the Holy Spirit who gives us that warning and alerts us not to make the wrong decision.

How many unnecessary things, bad moments, bad experiences, or tears could be avoided if we listened to that voice within us; but we all fail in one way or another. No one in this life is perfect. The key is repentance and forgiveness. I will touch on those topics in more depth later but let me just get ahead a little. God is a God of love and forgiveness. He knows your heart; He knows when you are sincere. The only thing He is waiting for is for you to acknowledge your error, repent, and not do it again.

Bad habits blind us and poison us. They damage us from the inside out. They make us into people we no longer recognize. When this happens, we become bearers of hatred, evil, sadness, division, and enmity. We go around the world by spreading our evil vibes to others causing harm, not only in ourselves, but everyone around us. It is never too late – listen to that voice that is alerting you.

"There is no fear in love. But perfect love drives out fear, because fear has to do with punishment. The one who fears is not made perfect in love."
(1 John 4:18 NIV)

CHAPTER 3

My Family Went from Five to Three

T he months went by, and my family and I started to go through a very difficult time, especially my mom. By that time, my dad was diagnosed with an incurable disease and my sister, Adriana became pregnant at the age of eighteen. She made the decision to marry and leave our home to create her own.

Now, my mom found herself trying to hold together a home that felt as if a hurricane was hitting it. My mother, Maria Sylvia, has always been a woman of a strong character and with her feet well placed on the ground when making decisions. She is not a woman to show love with a lot of physical affection or words, but she does it in her own way; a way we understand. The only thing my mother could do at that time was to use a lot of strength and put herself to work to provide for her husband, who was constantly in the hospital for treatment, and for the two daughters she had left at home.

My mom had always been a housewife. Since I was young, she made the decision to stay home taking care of me and my sisters. Although she was a college graduate, she preferred to dedicate herself to her family and give us her best...time and love. My mom has always been a warrior; never letting the circumstances of life scare her or defeat her, especially with the specific situation she was facing.

My parents always taught us the importance of educating ourselves and becoming professionals. One of their main focuses was to teach us to become people who will change a society where values are being lost. Although we were never a family to go to church or congregate weekly, we were taught about the fear and respect to God as a divine and sovereign being. My dad, Adrian Gamaliel, was a man who despite his strong character, always showed his feelings. He was incredibly open with us and mom. He was also a writer and a poet, never denying us the opportunity to write and teach us to passionately love words that became paragraphs through writing. He also did not miss the opportunity to always give us a life lesson. He was a genius. He did everything from working in gardens to working on cars. My dad was the life of the party, full of life and joy. Despite having had a difficult past, my parents always showed us love and taught us the importance of maintaining unity as a family, no matter what. I always saw my parents showing love to each other, even if their relationship was not always picture perfect. They were always together until my dad's last breath. Unfortunately, he could not win the battle of his illness and died in November 1994.

Now it was just my mom, my younger sister, Sylvia Liani, who was ten years old, and me. My mom had no other choice but to work to support her small family of three. There was a time after my dad died that we were homeless. We had to turn the keys in of the rented house where we lived. So, my mom, even with the pain of losing her husband, had the added stress of not having a roof to provide for her daughters. She managed to find an exceedingly small one-bedroom apartment last minute, where only my younger sister and her could fit. In her desperation, she spoke to my older sister to see if I could stay in her extra bedroom in her apartment while she was able to stabilize herself economically. My sister agreed without any hesitation, so I ended up living with her.

THE EFFECT OF A LOSS

To this day, I cannot understand or explain why I cannot remember in detail the time of pain and everything we went through as a family during my dad's illness. I am not a psychologist, but my subconscious created a self-protection mechanism that numbed me of anything that could destroy me. I do remember the pain of the loss, but, even if it sounds harsh or insensitive, I do not remember crying or suffering a lot after his death; it is like at this time, my memory was erased. Many of my memories of that time I deleted completely. Not because I wanted to, but I just do not remember. Even if I tried to remember, I cannot seem to manage to do so. However, now as an adult, I cry every time I remember my dad and the memories, I have of him when he was healthy. I miss him so much and I cannot wait for the time to see him again when we are in heaven. One of the greatest satisfactions I have is to know that my sister, Adriana, managed to present him the plan of salvation on his deathbed, which he accepted.

The feeling of loss is one that we all experience at some point in our lives. The effect on each person varies for different reasons, but everyone experiences the feeling of emptiness to some extent. In my case, the loss of my dad and the loss of the family structure I knew (my mom, dad, and my two sisters living in the same household) caused a negative effect on me. Now as an adult and mentally healthy, I can recognize that much of the bad decisions I made in my youth were due to the lack of love and attention of a paternal figure and the sudden emptiness I felt from the rupture of my family nucleus.

We all go through difficult situations, but sometimes we think we are the only ones going through pain. We sink into our darkness or sometimes focus on the strategies we will use to survive, forgetting those around us, who also suffer with us and like us.

It is important to talk, vent, and seek help. It is important not to make fast decisions when we are hurt or offended. We must learn to practice love, even in the difficult moments when we do not want to give it. Bad actions change our lives and those around us. This reminds me of the story of David and King Saul. If you do not know it, I invite you to read it in the first book of Samuel in the Bible. This story explains how David, who was called from an early age by God to be king and defeated a giant with a stone and a simple sling, demonstrated the importance of making decisions based on love, even when love was not reciprocated. The story states that David began a beautiful friendship and brotherhood with King Saul's son, Jonathan, who motivated the king to invite him to stay with them. The king also learned to love him in such a manner that David thought of him as a father. King Saul had trusted David so much that he practically became his right-hand man in every aspect throughout the kingdom. One day, after David returned from battle with his army, they were greeted by all the women of different cities of Israel shouting, dancing, and singing "Saul killed his thousands, and David killed his tens of thousands!"

This infuriated Saul to the point where his love turned into hatred, resulting in David being persecuted by King Saul for years. Saul's obsession with David led him to the point where he threw him out of the palace and tried to kill him on several occasions. Imagine the horrible pain that David felt. The man he loved, who he considered a father and a mentor, now sought to kill him tirelessly. The pain David experienced was so great that it brought him to the edge of madness.

David had many opportunities to avenge Saul, even the opportunity to kill him, but he never did. Why? Because David always understood that he did not have the right to judge, only God. David knew that despite everything, Saul was still the anointed of God. This made him respect. Him and fear the Lord to the end. Wow! What a strong and incredible thought that a man might think like this after all that he had experienced. David was acting in love; a love that is supernatural and that can only be understood when we meet the source of that love, God.

Today I invite you to reflect on your situations. You are not alone. There is someone who cares and watches for you always, someone who puts people around you to help you overcome what you are going through. Try to understand that you are not the only one going through a season. At times where you need to be loved, I urge you to practice giving love, even if you do not want to do it. The outcome of sacrifices like this will always have a positive reflection.

Many do not understand this concept of "Give without waiting for anything in return." We live in a society that teaches us that love is conditional; give only when we receive it in return. Therefore, when we act contrary to what the world believes, we are looked at as being crazy. If God is love and we are called His children and His most precious creation, then love is part of our DNA.

"See what great love the Father has lavished on us, that we should be called children of God! And that is what we are! The reason the world does not know us is that it did not know him." (1 John 3: 1 NIV)

CHAPTER 4

Our First Kiss

My encounters with Chapi were sporadic. He always tried to find a reason to see me, but always had the excuse of our siblings in the middle. One example of these excuses was the day I celebrated my fifteenth birthday. I never liked the traditional "quinceañeros" (a traditional Hispanic celebration usually for girls turning fifteen), so I celebrated my fifteenth birthday at home. I just invited my closest friends and some of my cousins. The party was not big since we were just going through the recent loss of my dad. We could not keep having additional expenses either because I had just arrived from a trip from New York, where I had gone to be a maid of honor for my cousin's wedding. So, we kept everything simple and small.

That day, when the party was nearing an end, Chapi showed up with one of his friends. His excuse to come over was that he was going to meet with Abraham, who was going to give him some money for working with him since both Abraham and Chapi were independent wood workers. If that were really the reason, he would have stayed in the car and would not have dressed as cute as he did. When I heard his car come through my street- Chapi has always modified the exhausts of his cars- automatically I knew it was him and I told one of my friends, "Chapi is coming. I will be right back." I went to my room to look out my window to see if it was him. Once I knew, I waited for him to come into the living room. I did not want to make it obvious, so I waited a few minutes in my room and then returned to the party.

That day I had put on a very "beachy" dress that my mom had given me. The dress was of bohemian style. I wore my hair loosely so that my curls would be accented more from the hairstyle. When I came out of my room, Chapi was in the living room in front of Abraham. He was speaking to him and had his back towards the hallway where I came from. I remember that when he saw me, he could not hide his smile, one that covered his whole face. It stunned me that he did not even try to hide it. I went to him and greeted him. He told me in front of his brother, "Wow, you look so pretty!" You cannot imagine the embarrassment I felt. That day we took pictures together; pictures that I still have to this day.

On another occasion, my family hosted a meeting at my aunt's house to do an activity in memory of my dad. That was a very emotional night for everyone. When the celebration of my dad's life was almost done, Chapi arrived. When I heard his car in the distance, I went to my sister Adriana and asked her if Chapi was coming. She said yes because Abraham had to give him money for working with him. I got incredibly nervous like I used to get whenever I saw him.

I remember seeing them talk through a door that was open and that was perfectly aligned right in front of where he had parked. He stayed in his car while Abraham talked to him. After they finished talking, Abraham came back in the house, but Chapi did not leave. Abraham got close to me and told me that Chapi wanted to speak with me. I went and asked mom for permission to go outside and speak to him, to which she allowed me to do. When I went out to his car, I opened the car door and I sat in the passenger seat. In my house, we were taught that a woman should never lay against or wait outside of a car where a man was sitting in, since this was what prostitutes used to do; this lesson has stayed with me since.

When I sat down, he told me that he was sorry for the loss of my dad. I began to cry, and he hugged me. That moment led us to our first kiss. It was an unforgettable moment. He was very gentle and careful while kissing me. I could feel his love and care for me. It lasted a little time because I felt bad about what I was doing, especially at a time when my family and I were going through the pain of my dad's loss. I asked him to forgive me and left.

THE ILLUSION OF LOVE

At some point in your life, you should have experienced the feeling of being in love. But if you have not experienced it yet, let me tell you that it is the most beautiful and inexplicable feeling a person may feel. There are no words that can explain it because it is magical. The rollercoaster of emotions of seeing the person you want are examples of the wonderful effect that love can provoke. Those butterflies in the belly, those sweaty hands, the uncontrollable nerves, the desperation of wanting to see him/her and to be close to him/her all the time, the thought that he/she is perfect (even though you know he/she is not), the unexplained joy that produces his/her simple smile, the inexhaustible thoughts day and night that make you lose your concentration… In short, there are so many qualities, I could write another book by giving you examples of the physical reactions produced by the feeling of love.

Have you ever wondered how love was created or where it was born? Love is not created, but rather, love is born in us in an intimate way. You will say, "How?" In the previous chapter, I mentioned to you that love is in our DNA because God is love and we are His children and His most precious creation.

Have you ever seen a baby smile when he sees or hears the voice of his parents or a child of color playing with another white-skinned child without any impairment or racial discrimination? These examples are some that show us that we were born with the ability to love.

The love that we possess naturally is one that is thin and conditioned. Allow me to explain myself. When you love, naturally you must feed it and take care of it because it can be easily affected. Now, the love we receive from God is a supernatural love; it is an infinite and unconditional love. It is a love that is always hopeful and always perseveres. The Word says:

"Love is patient, love is kind. It does not envy, it does not boast, it is not proud. It does not dishonor others, it is not self-seeking, it is not easily angered, it keeps no record of wrongs. Love does not delight in evil but rejoices with the truth. It always protects, always trusts, always hopes, always perseveres."
(1 Corinthians 13: 4-7 NIV)

According to the Greeks, there are four types of love. The first love is **eros.** This love represents the passionate and erotic love, characterized by experiencing physical, sexual, and instinctive attraction. The second love is **storge**. This love represents a fraternal, friendly, and committed love. It is characterized by being a loyal and protective love. This type of love develops over time. The third love is **philia**. This love is also found among friends and love for your neighbor, seeking the common good. This love is characterized by being a selfless love. The fourth love is **agape**. The Greeks called this love the purest and most unconditional love that exists. Agape love does not seek its own pleasure, but it finds satisfaction in giving love.

This last one is found only in God. It is through Him that we understand its true meaning and can bring its essence into action. This love is a supernatural one and therefore, we must seek to nourish it, care for it, and seek it every day in the same way we do with the other types of love; for our sinful ways separates us from Him. Living lives committed to God develops the ability to love as Jesus did because we model what we receive from Him when we are in His presence.

So, if we can experience and feel so many wonderful things for another person, imagine how much more our heavenly Father feels for us. His love is inexplicable and inexhaustible. Believe that every time He looks at us, He cannot help but smile.

CHAPTER 5

Not a Goodbye but a See You Later

Time passed and I tried to cope with the new reality of life without my dad. One day, Adriana brought the baby, Abraham Jr., so we could see him. I remember her sharing that Chapi was going to live with his older sister and his mother in the state of Vermont in the United States. I cried a lot, but I never called or tried to go see him.

Weeks before they left, Chapi surprised me and showed up at my house. He had brought me a necklace with a wooden cross. The necklace was made of little metal balls like the ones that soldiers often use, better known as their dog tags or identification tags. At that time, they were in style, and he had learned from Abraham that I have been wanting to get one just like the one my sister had. I went outside to greet him with an embarrassed smile, like the one he had. He had come in his dad's truck; he did not get out from it. I remember his expression when he saw me walking toward him. He had lowered the window, put his head out and leaned over the window with his arms crossed waiting for me to get to the truck. As I got closer, he opened one of his hands where he hid the necklace and then let it hang from one of his fingers.

When I saw him, I began to laugh and said, "How did you know I wanted one?" He answered, "I always figure out a way to know everything that has to do with you." I told him that I had found out that they were moving and that I could not believe it. He replied that it was a decision that his mother had made to help his older sister who was a single mother. I replied that I was going to miss him for the rest of my life and that I was never going to forget him. He replied, "I promise you that we will see each other again." I turned around and started walking back to the house while my tears started to run down my face.

Every night I looked at the photos that we took when we first met. I always wore the necklace that he gave me without worrying if it matched my clothes. Every chance I had I would ask Abraham about him. I remember one of the times he replied to me, "Girl, he is driving all the "gringas" (American girls) crazy at school! He is the only one with dark skin and all those blondes are in love with him and the other guys are jealous. Chapi tells me that every day he finds notes the girls leave in his locker, desk, or his car." Those words were rumbling in my mind like a big echo in the Grand Canyon. I remember that night I cried a lot because I thought I had lost him. To my surprise, three months later Chapi and his family returned to Puerto Rico (ha, ha, ha… so much crying for nothing).

GOD KNOWS THE DESIRES OF YOUR HEART

It feels so good to receive a gift, especially when it is something you have always wanted. In my case, everyone in my family knows that I treasure the simple things more, especially if they are letters written by them. I have always loved letters and they have an incredibly noteworthy value for me.

The value of a gift is not given by the item, but by the intention with which it is given. Sometimes we want gifts to fill voids that an object cannot provide. So many times, unnecessary things are given away to disguise a feeling of disappointment, lack of love, or attention. Those gifts may be treasured at that moment, but they will never fill the heart. They become layers of soil that are thrown to cover a broken pipe that leaks water. You cannot see it, but it is still broken. The simple presence of a person that is in a theater recital, which will be held at the same time as an important work reunion, will cause a greater effect and surprise on the person that needed to know that it was more important than any reunion in the world. The gift's value is in the intention of which it is given, while the satisfaction is of the gift's intentions.

Other times we think we need things; sometimes we crave them and sometimes we even become obsessed with them. When we receive a gift, we think that is what we want so much, but when we open it, it was not what we wanted and disappointment is inevitable. Our reactionns, words, and expressions are not always the best when we receive gifts. Sometimes they demonstrate a lack of gratitude, even when you know that the gift will have a more valuable use compared to the item you really wanted

33

to receive. The reality is that many times we want things that we do not need.

However, when I received the necklace that Chapi gave me, what moved me the most was not the object, but knowing that he knew what I needed, not what I wanted. I needed his attention and his gesture of love, not the necklace. His words confirmed my feelings when I asked him how he knew what I wanted by saying **"I always figure out a way to know everything that has to do with you."**

Wow! God is the same way. He is always watching out for us; He knows what we need, not what we want. Sometimes when we ask God for things, we cry, pray, and ask Him to grant us our request, then get disappointed because we never received it. This is not because God could not give it to us, but because He knew that was not what we needed. Disappointment could be avoided if our focus had not been in the petition, but in the One who makes it possible. What a better example than Jesus himself; while knowing that He was going to be crucified, knowing that He was innocent, letting His Father know what He wanted, but asking Him to give Him what was necessary.

"He withdrew about a stone's throw beyond them, knelt down and prayed, 'Father, if you are willing, take this cup from me; yet not my will, but yours be done.' An angel from heaven appeared to him and strengthened him."
(Luke 22: 41-43 NIV)

When we ask the Father, let us do so in trust, but always keeping in mind that His will is done first.

"And this is the confidence that we have toward him, that if we ask anything according to his will he hears us."
(1 John 5:14 ESV)

CHAPTER 6

His Last Girlfriend

Sometime later, Chapi met a girl who had attended my school and was Adriana's friend as well; she was beautiful. She was in her fourth year of high school, but she did not finish because she got pregnant. Chapi met her while she was in her last months of pregnancy, yet he began a relationship with her. This was something that made me incredibly angry. Every time I saw him with his girlfriend, I was dying of jealousy. I tried to act and hide as if I did not care what he was doing or who he was with. I know there were times where it bothered him to see my attitude, but both of us tried to disguise it. Every time he found out I was also talking or dating someone, he would show up at my home like some sort of magic trick looking for an excuse to cover his obvious visit.

It was always like that; when he was with someone, I suffered and when I was with someone, it was him who suffered. Abraham used to ask him why he did not ask me to be his girlfriend. The answer Chapi used to give him was, "Socio," (nickname that they as brothers used which translates to partner) I know that she and I are going to end up getting married, but now is not the time to be together." Even his friends used to tell him the same thing. He felt so confident about my feelings for him that he had made the decision to choose when to be or not to be with me; something that we both had a habit of doing.

The months passed by, and I began to realize that their relationship became increasingly serious. I saw how he started to become the father of her baby, leaving me to feel as if I was being forgotten. Then I found out they had decided to live together; I felt powerless and desperate.

One day Adriana invited me to the beach with them. Chapi is the youngest of four siblings. That day they all went, including Chapi's girlfriend. I remember that no one in the family liked that relationship. Everyone wanted him to be with me. I do not remember exactly why, but I ended up riding with her to the beach that day. When we arrived at the beach, we found an empty parking spot which was in the middle of two cars. She spent more than 10 minutes trying to reverse her car into the spot and she was not able to do it. She was embarrassed because they were all coming down the sidewalk walking with all their bags and coolers to the beach, and she had not even managed to park yet. I was already getting desperate and the only thing she said was, "If Chapi were here, he would have parked it a long time ago." As soon as she said that my blood began to boil from anger. I could not hold it anymore and as, I opened the door, I said, "Get out and let me park it." She laughed because she thought I was also going to make a fool of myself, so she accepted. As soon as I closed the driver's door, I parked the car in less than a minute. At that time, I thanked my dad in my mind for teaching me to park in reverse before I learned to drive.

By this time, everyone got to her car and saw what was going on, including Chapi, who looked at me and smiled; making me feel like he was proud of me. The girl was upset by what happened. This uncomfortable situation motivated her to find any reason to seek an opportunity to mortify me. She had her first chance that same day on our way back home while talking to Adriana about their plans to get married. When I heard her, my stomach fluttered and I wanted to vomit. I got so angry that I could not hold it and that same night I sent a message to Chapi on the "beeper" (also known as a pager, a device of the ninety's where you received text messages sent through an operator who you had to call by telephone).

The message said something like this, "I cannot believe you have come to the extreme of wanting to get married. I feel so disappointed with you. Att. Zuanía." I thought he would call to give me an explanation, but he did not. At least that day he did not. I went to sleep full of rage and crying.

Days later, I remember that I was at his mom's house with Adriana and Abraham because they had invited us to eat. Out of nowhere, I heard his car arrive. At that time, I did not know if he lived there or with his girlfriend because they always spent their time fighting and leaving each other. Every time they broke up, he picked up his things and brought them back home to his parents.

Now we laugh when we remember those times because I tell him that he had come to a point of being like the nomads. He always had his belongings in his car so that he did not have to overwork by taking it out since he did not know if the status of his relationship would change. Finally, when I heard his car arrive, I was extremely nervous because I remembered the message, the one that I spoke of earlier.

I wanted to know if he was going to have the guts to answer me. When he came in, he greeted everyone, except me. That made me even more angry, I almost cried, but I held it together. His mom asked him if he was going to eat, which he said no, because he had only come over to look for something.

When he came downstairs, I was watching TV in the living room. When he saw that I was alone he approached me and said, "How are you?" Since I was angry, I said, "Now you want to say hi and speak to me. Now when there is no one, right? Of course, because it has always been like that. You only look for me when you want, everything must be hidden, and I am always so dumb that I follow the game." Well, as they say back home, "I gave him a piece of my mind." He responded ashamedly, "I know how angry you are Zuanía, but calm down, I am not getting married. Those are lies from that maniac (referring to his girlfriend). You know she said it to bother you." He always knew the words I wanted or needed to hear to calm me down. When he told me that he took his keys and left.

THE SPIRITUAL AND ACADEMIC EDUCATION
Today I can see everything I have lived in my life so far. I realize the great need for mentors or spiritual guides to speak to us and help us make wise decisions during those teenage years.

I can see the importance of ***Proverbs 22:6 (ESV)*** where it says, ***"Train up a child in the way he should go; even when he is old, he will not depart from it."***

I was taught in other areas where values and education were the priority, something I will always be forever grateful to my parents, but I never had someone to guide me spiritually and teach me the truth of God. God certainly had mercy on us and always kept us in His hands. Now that we are parents, we see the difference in leading our children through God's way and making those spiritual values first in our lives.

It is important to recognize that both academic and spiritual learning go hand in hand, especially during the years of youth where our identity is questioned and leads us to define who we are and what we believe in. That is the moment our spiritual mentors play a particularly significant role in our lives. My dad used to tell me that the places we would spend our time would determine who we would be and even who we would marry. In other words, the influence of our surroundings affects our character and our decisions.

If we do not balance these two educations, we will always be uneven. Human knowledge and wisdom are successful when we focus on God. When we do not understand this, we will simply be wise with human knowledge and will be easily persuaded with any innovative ideas that are presented to us. The wisdom that comes from God is one that gives us security, stability, and positive results. In Him, we find peace, the understanding of how perfect He is, and how imperfect we are.

"Who is wise and understanding among you? Let them show it by their good life, by deeds done in the humility that comes from wisdom. But if you harbor bitter envy and selfish ambition in your hearts, do not boast about it or deny the truth. Such 'wisdom' does not come down from heaven but is earthly, unspiritual, demonic. For where you have envy and selfish ambition, there you find disorder and every evil practice. But the wisdom that comes from heaven is first of all pure; then peace-loving, considerate, submissive, full of mercy and good fruit, impartial and sincere. Peacemakers who sow in peace reap a harvest of righteousness."
(James 3:13-18 NIV)

CHAPTER 7

A Toxic Relationship

Iwas a member of the Honor Roll, part of the volleyball team in my school and a team in my community called Avoli. I was always a dedicated student, but I liked to talk a lot; a habit that took me to the principal's office to be disciplined multiple times. I remember that on numerous occasions, I interrupted class to run to the window and watch Chapi go by with his car, which I could hear from a distance. My classroom had a view to the beach and Chapi knew it. Every time he was going or just finished surfing, he had a habit of passing by the street of my school and accelerating the car to let me know that he was passing by. This happened every day. At first it brought me many problems with the teachers, but then they got used to it and laughed each time he did it. They let me watch for a few seconds and then they would tell me to sit. Therewere times when my friends and I would be bold enough to skip classes; we jumped the fence that was facing the beach and we would leave. It was usually days when the waves were good, and the beach was filled with surfers. Many of my friends jumped to go see the impressive waves, but I did it to go see Chapi surf.

By that time, Chapi was fighting with his girlfriend every day. He did not like the lifestyle she was living. Despite everything, Chapi was very calm. He did not usually go to clubs and when he did, he did not drink alcohol. There were very few times when he did drink, and it was mostly because he wanted to experience it or simply because he felt peer pressure after his girlfriend and him went through a big fight. Chapi was the same way with smoking and using drugs; he never used them. He was well distinguished between his friends because of his actions and because his friends respected him, they did not usually smoke or use drugs around him.

One day we were at the beach and Abraham asked his sister Kivin why Chapi did not go. She told us that the previous day Chapi and his girlfriend had an unbelievably bad fight to the point where she had to intervene. They were in front of the house shouting at each other. According to Kivin, Chapi was shouting to his girlfriend to leave him alone for the last time and that he no longer wanted to have anything to do with her. She told us that he got in his car to leave, and that the girl threw herself over the hood of his car, preventing him from driving. He began to laugh because he could not believe to the extent that she had gone. During all that chaos, Chapi began calling Kivin from his car. When she opened one of the windows on the second floor, he yelled at her to please come down and help him remove the psycho from his car. As soon as she closed the window and came downstairs, Chapi's girlfriend got off of his car. Kivin told us that she approached the girl, picked up her purse from the floor, and asked her to get in her car and leave. She immediately obeyed to avoid any confrontation with her. His girlfriend also threatened him with ending her life, like his first girlfriend used to do. That was something specifically that scared him, especially because he thought about her daughter.

STAY AWAY FROM PEOPLE THAT DON'T SUIT YOU

In the previous chapter I mentioned how the place and the people we surround ourselves with are very influential for us in making decisions. These play a particularly significant role in our identity. For those of us who live lives to please God, we know that it becomes more difficult to identify what is best for us; for the battle to do something that I do not want to do is fought daily. Dependence on God is an action that involves practice and determination. Whenever you can sideline your wants and needs that will bring dire consequences to those around you, the results are always rewarding.

When I had no relationship with God, I lived a life where I functioned as others. My decisions and attitudes reflected a diseased society where values are put second. The influence of people, fashion, music, and lifestyles are crucial in the development of our identity. This does not mean that it is bad; what it means is that we must be wise with what we choose.

There are things and people who simply do not bring anything good to our lives. On the contrary, they destroy us, and it is often so slow that we do not realize it. Stay away from anything that does not help you develop the best you. Your best version will always be found in the reflection of God's mirror.

CHAPTER 8

The Temptation

One night, while we watched movies at Chapi's family's house, I asked him, "What's the miracle that brings you here with us?" He answered, "You already know." He was referring to what we both knew...that he was fighting with his girlfriend and that they had broken up again. I looked at him while shaking my head, demonstrating the disbelief that he kept going on in such a toxic relationship and said, "Wow, Chapi when will it stop?"

He had sat by my side, which he took advantage of to grab my hand without anyone realizing it. He would rub my hand gently and occasionally squeeze it tight as if he were trying to say what he felt for me and that I was the one he wanted to be with. We held hands for about 10 minutes, which I stopped doing because I remembered about our whole history and how we had created the habit of doing these things.

I moved my hand a bit aggressively as I looked at him and moved my head saying 'no,' without talking so others did not notice. Although he was embarrassed, he respected my decision because he knew I was right.
The first movie we were watching finished. Everyone took

advantage of the time and went to the bathroom or downstairs to eat something before starting the next movie. At that moment, he told me that he was sleepy and that he was going to go to sleep on the couch in the living room so that I could stay in his room. That night, I slept over at his house because it was already late, and my sister could not take me home. Before he left, he said, "If you get thirsty, hungry, or cold, you know I'm going to be downstairs on the couch if you need anything." Even though he said it jokingly, I knew he wanted me to go look for him.

When we were in the middle of the second movie I was completely disconnected from my reality. I do not remember which movie we watched or what it was about. I lost my concentration after he told me he was going to be waiting downstairs. The only thing I could do was battle with my thoughts of whether I was going downstairs or not. What do you think I did? Exactly…I went downstairs.

When I was going downstairs, I realized that he was already laying down. I remember that the couch they had was next to the staircase. He had an arm on his face, as he usually does when he is falling asleep. He realized that I was approaching and began to laugh saying, "Uh, oh." He was a little scared because he knew something was going to happen.

We both laughed with caution so that no one would realize it. I sat on the couch where he was lying. I was motivating him to quickly sit in a position where we could be face to face. We stared at each other for a few minutes while we were smiling. He took my hands and then dropped them quickly due to the mental battle he was also experiencing. With one of his hands, he put some of the hair that had come off my ponytail and fell on one side of my face behind my ears. I took advantage, grabbed him, and rubbed his other hand that was close to mine. And that was when we kissed.

Although we liked what we were doing, we knew it was wrong. I remember seeing tears come down Chapi's cheeks while kissing me. I knew he was feeling guilty because even though he was separated from his girlfriend at that time, he knew it was not definite. When I saw him like that, I stepped back and asked for forgiveness, which he did as well. He confessed that he wanted to be with me and wanted to continue kissing me, but he knew that it was not the time. He did not want to continue doing things the wrong way because if one day we started a relationship, he wanted to do it right. As he told me those words, he stroked my face with his hand. I understood and respected his way of thinking, for it was the same thing that I thought. I lowered his hand which was still on my face. I left and I went upstairs; I heard him crying in the background. Every time I remember that image, my heart breaks with sadness

THE FIGHT AGAINST SIN
"I do not understand what I do. For what I want to do I do not do, but what I hate I do. And if I do what I do not want to do, I agree that the law is good. As it is, it is no longer I myself who do it, but it is sin living in me. For I know that good itself does not dwell in me, that is, in my sinful nature. For I have the desire to do what is good, but I cannot carry it out. For I do not do the good I want to do, but the evil I do not want to do—this I keep on doing. Now if I do what I do not want to do, it is no

longer I who do it, but it is sin living in me that does it. So, I find this law at work: Although I want to do good, evil is right there with me. For in my inner being I delight in God's law; but I see another law at work in me, waging war against the law of my mind and making me a prisoner of the law of sin at work within me. What a wretched man I am! Who will rescue me from this body that is subject to death?" **(Romans 7: 15-24 *NIV*)**

Wow! I believe that after these verses there is not much to abound. This chapter of Romans is one of my favorites because it perfectly describes how I feel everyday with my own battles. Paul, being one of the disciples and having walked beside Jesus, experienced it just like I did. Temptation is an extraordinarily strong feeling; it was what we experienced in our teenage years, unaware of what would be unleashed in the spiritual world if and when we allow sin to enter.

"Blessed is the man that endureth temptation: for when he is tried, he shall receive the crown of life, which the Lord hath promised to them that love him."
(James 1:12 KJV)

These situations happen daily, not only with young people, but with adults as well. Sexual life is one that God created, but it was designed to be enjoyed within marriage. Perhaps, you are reading this as a young man or woman and think that all you have read so far is a love story that is being told in an exciting and joking way, along with the adventures we have been through. Yes, there were exciting experiences that we would not change, but there are many other things that we would like to go back in time and change the way we handled them.

God created the stages of our lives so that each one will be enjoyed in their own time. When we want to skip those stages and enjoy things that belong to other stages, everything is distorted. God is a God of order. He is the creator of order; He knows when we are ready to live and experience certain things. When we are not able to wait and we skip the divine order, we damage the original plans that God had for us. Believe me, His plans are better than you could imagine. I tell you this from experience. Later, I will share the consequences that we had to go through by allowing sin to enter our lives and make incorrect decisions that ruined the original plan that God had designed for us as a couple.

Perhaps, you are an adult, and you see that there are many factors you can analyze when reading this story. You may have seen the ignorance and immaturity of both in certain situations and you may have also seen an early teen behave inappropriately, or even ask yourself where their parents were when all of this was happening. I could write many wise words to you that would justify our actions, but that is not what I want. I want you to understand that the spiritual world does exist, that heaven is real, but darkness is also real and that above all things, there is a lion looking for whom to devour. I cannot question God's sovereignty and the way things were given in my life. If I am sure of something, it is that when a human being lives a life away from their Creator and His plans, they live with a constant emptiness. When this emptiness or void is detected, people try to fill it with everything this world offers: money, careers, relationships, sex, drugs, and even religions. I assure you that everyone at some point in our short stay in this universe will meet the One who created it all for us because of love. God is a God of perfect times. He already knows when it will be our time to meet Him, even if that encounter comes in a way that we do not understand now. It will be at that very moment that we have the responsebility to make the decision that brings us closer to or further away from Him. Every human, in some way or another, base our decisions on how we will benefit from them. I assure you that if you decide to get closer to Him, the result will always be good, even in the most difficult situations you face.

CHAPTER 9

I Met a New Love

everal weeks passed and I had made the decision to forget Chapi completely. I wanted to take him out of my life because I understood that the relationship, we had created was toxic. I had reached a point where I was only affecting myself emotionally to the extent that it began to reflect in my grades at school, something that was extremely important to me.

Adriana and Abraham began to attend a church that Mara (Chapi's older sister) and Aidita Perez (now my mother-in-law), as I called her out of love, invited them to. One day, Adriana invited me to attend church with them and told me that it was going to be an arts night and that I would like it. I did not understand what she meant by that. She tried to explain it to me by comparing it with a talent show. That caught my attention because for many years I belonged to a group where we used to present ourselves in talent shows and competitions with wind instruments. I am not going to lie...my biggest interest was to know if I had a chance to see Chapi.

I remember getting to the church parking lot, searching all around for Chapi's car and realizing he was not there. The feelings that I had been battling with for those past weeks came back strongly to torment me, making me feel that I was alone and lacking in love.

That is how the enemy works, by tormenting us and deceiving us. It makes us feel that the situation we are currently experiencing is the definite one and that there is no hope. Oh, but God is good, for He comes at the perfect moment.

As soon as I opened the doors of the church and began to see and listen to the lyrics of the song that they were using for a dance recital, I felt something that entered my heart and filled me with a love that I had never experienced. A love that made me feel complete and important. Tears began to come down my cheeks and I could not understand what was happening to me. They were tears of joy for something or someone that made me feel loved right at that precise moment. At that time, I could not understand what was happening to me and I felt a lot of shame because I did not want people to see me like that. I thought I was going to be told that I was crazy.

Today I know that what I felt at that time was the fullness of the Holy Spirit who came to my life at the tender age of fifteen. He came to fill me with the perfect and incomparable love that we only find in God. Today I laugh because at that time I thought that all those around me were going to tell me I was crazy. What I did not know was that I was surrounded by many crazy people. It says in
1 Corinthians 1:18 (KJV): "For the preaching of the cross is to them that perish foolishness; but unto us which are saved it is the power of God."

Those crazy people felt and experienced the same thing I was feeling. From that day on, I began to visit the church weekly with my sister and her husband. I began to engage with the young people in all their activities and ministries. My life changed completely. I saw life differently and felt different. Even though I still had feelings for Chapi, I was no longer affected and I could feel peace now.

I began to develop and understand what it was to wait on God. I prayed for Chapi every day. Now my prayer was that he could find the love that I had found. I prayed that God would fulfill His will in him, but that He would help him make the best decisions that would transform his life. One day I was getting ready to evangelize in the streets of Old San Juan. This activity had been planned by church leaders and youth. There we would also take advantage to celebrate my sixteenth birthday. In the weeks leading up to this event, I was spending some time with a boy from the church. He asked me if he could pick me up for us to leave together to the event, which I accepted.

That night Adriana and Abraham came over to eat at home and bring their boys to spend some time with us at our house. By that time, my other nephew Sebastian had been born. After spending some time with them, I left so I could shower and begin getting ready. The boy said he would pick me up at 7:00 p.m. and it was already 6:00 p.m. While I was showering, I thought I heard a car like Chapi's, but I ignored it because I thought it was just my imagination. When I got out of the bathroom, I heard Abraham talking to someone and to my surprise, I realized that it was him. I went quickly to my room and when I closed the door, I started talking to God. I asked Him why He had allowed him to be there that day, at that precise moment. My heart started to beat fast as I became super nervous because of the feelings I still had for him. I knew with him being there, he was going to find out I was going out with someone else, and I did not know how my friend was going to react when he found out that this was the famous Chapi, who I had spoken about earlier. No one in my house knew I was talking to that young man, not even my sister. I had made the decision to keep it a secret because I wanted to be sure of my feelings toward him and because I did not want Chapi to know.

So, I got out of my room all dressed up and everyone was all surprised, except for my mom, who obviously knew I was going out. I remember Chapi's expression; he could not help but smile and he did not take his eyes off me. It was a very difficult encounter for both of us, as we had not seen each other for a long time. My sister asked me where I was going, and I replied that I was going to the outing with the youth from the church. She asked me who was going to pick me up. That was the question I was trying to avoid, but I filled myself with courage and answered. When I finished telling her his name, she asked me the other question that I did not want her to specifically ask me in front of Chapi, "Are you guys going out as a couple?" I looked at her with a facial epression as if to say, "Shut your mouth girl!" Something she completely ignored as she asked again. I had no other option but to answer her. I told her that we were not going out, but we were talking.

I returned to my room to wait to get picked up and get over my embarrassment. I thought by going to my room, Chapi would leave as he usually did when he got mad, but it did not happen like that. When my friend arrived, I went outside to open the gate for him. He had gotten out of the car to introduce himself to my mom and let her know that he would take me and bring me back home safely. When we entered the house, I introduced him to everyone, including Chapi. He was so upset that when my friend greeted him, he did not answer or even look at him. At this moment, my body felt ice cold from the embarrassment. I said goodbye to everyone, and we left.

When we were on our way, my friend asked me who the guy at my home was (referring to Chapi). I replied that he was the brother of my brother-in-law, the one who I had talked to him about before, trying not to go into details. He replied, "What? It seems like he did not like me." I took a deep breath and began to tell him more about our story. When I finished telling him about me and Chapi, he told me not to worry. He said that it was normal for him to feel like that, but that he would not miss the opportunity to be with a girl like me. I am not going to lie to you guys, the time I was talking and getting to know this boy I felt like little by little I was falling in love with him. Something that Chapi could notice that night as he watched us talk.

A month passed and I remember that one day Adriana asked me to take care of the boys at her house. I told her yes, but that mom could not take me. She told me not to worry because Chapi was going to work with Abraham and could take me. I sighed deeply because I knew I was exposed to conversations I did not want to have with him, but at the same time I was sure of myself and the good judgment I had developed in my relationship with God.

When Chapi arrived, he greeted me. I noticed he was nervous, but happy. I greeted him and then remained quiet, avoiding any conversation. I remember he was being a bit uneasy, like looking for a way to talk to me. Trying to ignore his attitude, I turned my head looking out of my window. I think that was what frustrated him the most because within a few minutes he broke the silence and said to me "Wow, to this extreme we have come that we cannot even speak?" I looked at him and replied, "I do not know why you say that. It is not that we cannot talk, I just do not want to talk to you." The tone I used was a calm one. I was transmitting a lot of peace but also a sense of security for myself. That was something he noticed because he quickly answered, "So it is true. You have changed so much. It is true what they have told me. If I liked you before, now I like you even more." I cannot lie, when he told me that it bothered me a little because I went back to the past. I asked God to give me the strength to remain at peace and answer him wisely.

I remember saying, "That is only God doing it," turning my head back toward my window. He replied that he was happy that I was attending church. He had considered starting to go more often. Since his mother began going to church, Chapi went to keep her company from time to time. He even went a few times when I was already attending weekly. He had always feared God, but at that time, attending church was not a priority. I told him that I was pleased that he had made that decision, but to please respect the fact that I was now talking to another person who deserves my respect as well. I asked him to let me redo my life because this time I wanted to do things right. I felt uncomfortable telling him this because despite everything, I felt like I still wanted him. However, I knew that if it were God's will for us to be together, things would be done right and in order. With that being said, I tried to not let myself be led by my emotions. I needed to die to my feelings to be able to please God with my actions.

He was surprised by this; he never thought I would reject him and especially in that way. He replied that he was going to respect me, but to please give him a last chance to tell me what was in his heart and that if after listening to him I still thought the same, he would turn away from me forever. He told me that the night he met my friend, he experienced a feeling he had never felt before. He confessed that besides the obvious jealousy he felt, he experienced how he lost me. It was a feeling that caused him a lot of fear. He acknowledged that he had always felt safe in the moments where it was just us because he knew that even though I was talking to someone else, I only had eyes for him. Now he knew I was with a person who had managed to divert my attention from him. He felt desperate because something inside him told him he was losing me. He started asking me to please give him a last chance; that if I did not really feel anything for him, he was going to understand and accept it, but if there were still feelings, I would reconsider my decision. He said to me with a trembling voice that he wanted me and that it was with me that he wanted to be with for the rest of his days.

As he spoke, I felt like my guard was coming down. I could not believe he was telling me all that. I wanted to cry and hugging him and telling him right away, but then I remembered his girlfriend and said, "C'mon now, you're telling me all this but what about your girlfriend?" He was confused and with a smile on his face he told me, "My girlfriend? You do not know? I left her a long time ago and since that day I have not seen her, nor have I spoken to her. After that night in your house something changed in me. I have not been able to stop thinking about you. A feeling of fear took a hold of me because I knew I was losing you."

I could not believe what I was hearing and much less, that I did not hear of that news. I started crying and confessed that I felt confused because even though I still had feelings for him, I was very afraid to fall back into a lifestyle like the one we had before. I shared my concern for my friend, of whom I was very fond. He told me that I did not have to decide at that time, but to please think about it and then let him know.

The following days were very difficult. I cried and prayed constantly. I knew what I wanted to do, but I was afraid to make the decision. Out of respect to my friend, I made the decision to stop seeing him. Even if I did not get back with Chapi, my friend did not deserve to be with me when I was not clear about my feelings. God made me understand that it was not right to use one person to forget another, even if I could have feelings for both.

A NAIL DOES NOT PULL ANOTHER NAIL
This is one of the biggest mistakes we make. We think that the saying, "A nail pulls another nail" is the best

alternative to forgetting another person, but it is not true. When you start a relationship, it must be when you both know and have the assurance that you are for each other. God does not want us to jump around looking for who our partner is going to be. God wants us to wait on Him. He knows the perfect time. He has our story written and knows when things will happen. So, it is on us to wait and be obedient because His plans are better than ours.

"'For my thoughts are not your thoughts, neither are your ways my ways,' declares the LORD. 'As the heavens are higher than the earth, so are my ways higher than your ways and my thoughts than your thoughts.'"
(Isaiah 55: 8-9 NIV)

Today I recognize that one of my biggest mistakes was not giving myself the credit that I deserved. When we do not understand how important we are to God and do not know how to value ourselves, we allow others to define us, which often leads to disappointments and failures. When we trust God and His timing, we rest in the hope of knowing that what we will receive will be even better than what we desire. Today I urge you to start seeing yourself as God sees you. He sees you as His greatest and best creation. We are the children of a King and as such, we must behave like royalty. Understand that you are worth a lot and that God loves you with unconditional love. Do not let anyone make you feel less.

"Jesus replied: 'Love the Lord your God with all your heart and with all your soul and with all your mind.' This is the first and greatest commandment. And the second is like it: 'Love your neighbor as yourself.' All the Law and the Prophets hang on these two commandments." (Matthew 22: 37-40 NIV)

CHAPTER 10
A New Beginning

I decided to end my sentimental relationship with the church boy. I stayed for several weeks alone, meditating, and waiting. Chapi began to go to church more often and became more involved with the youth group. Slowly we began to rebuild our relationship. He used to visit me at home after he left the beach. He would say that seeing me gave him energy. He was never one to talk on the phone. When he did, it was to ask me if he could come over. So, you can imagine how much he visited me. I asked him to call me, but he told me that he did not like to talk on the phone and that he preferred to talk face to face.

One day, while visiting me, he stared at me and simply said to me, "I love you so much. You are what I have always wanted." I felt like my whole skin got goosebumps…ha, ha, ha. I said, "We have been together for three months and I do not remember you officially asking me to be your girlfriend." He said that to him, we were a couple a long time ago. I know his answer was not one with bad intentions. He is a simple guy; he does not like protocols very much. I let him know what was in my heart and how important it was for me to hear him ask me to be his girlfriend. I thought that by hearing him ask me, it would unleash something in the spiritual sense where it would officially join us. He started laughing and told me, "If that makes you happy, then here it goes, Zuanía Molina, do you want to be my girlfriend?" I answered with a "Yeeeeeesss, at last!" From that day on, we have never separated again.

ORDER PRODUCES SATISFACTION

I am the type of person where a mess or disorganization produces stress. That is why I try to be orderly and organized with everything in my life. I am not perfect, so at times when I encounter a mess, regardless of how it was created, by someone else or myself, I do not allow it to reach the extreme of causing anxiety like it used to. This was a flaw that I had to work hard on. My anxiety caused me on many occasions to hurt others with my demands to maintain order and control of the situation that at that time, robbed me of my peace. I have improved a lot, but I know I have a long way to go. What I am sure of is that I am not the same person as before. Today I enjoy the satisfaction produced by the things I plan, without having the need to feel anxiety when I stumble upon obstacles that I will always encounter in my life.

I have learned to handle it in the same way I did with my relationship with Chapi because I gave it to God. Many times, doing the right thing is not easy. Most of the time it means that we must do things that we do not like or are not used to doing. When God's priorities become our priorities, life takes on more meaning; everything is more bearable, even when that way of life is sometimes impossible for many. God does not want us to live messy lives. He wants us to understand the satisfaction that order brings when we obey Him.

CHAPTER 11

A Pregnancy Not Planned

Even though during our relationship everything was good, we began to move away from God. Although we continued to attend church and fellowship with the youth, our relationship began to be our priority. We let our fleshly desires take over us, yielding to the temptation of having sex.

By that time, I lived at Adriana and Abraham's house. I think that made it more difficult and easier at the same time for us. Knowing that we were so close, that we had more freedom to see each other and meet whenever we wanted to, made it more attractive. We were young with our hormones on "high." One night I asked Chapi to take me to the Baskin Robbins Ice Cream Shop because I was craving an ice cream that they sold that had a brownie. I remember eating that ice cream like I would never eat it again. I enjoyed it and savored it so much that Chapi was staring at me confused, but above all worried. He began to suspect that I was pregnant. He did not want to tell me at that time because he was afraid to think it was true, but he did say it when he saw other more suspicious changes in my body. For example, one day he touched my belly and felt it was harder: a little sprout. Something that was more noticeable in me because at that time I weighed about ninety-eight pounds. I was super skinny. The days passed and I experienced more changes in my body. I felt that every time I did the abdominal exercises in volleyball practices, it bothered me and caused me some pain. Every time Adriana cooked bean stew, I had to lock myself in my room because the smell made me nauseous. Those were the reasons that made me open my eyes and realize that Chapi's suspicions were true. I did not take my period into consideration because it used to be very irregular. There were times I could be up to two months without menstruating. The problem was that I had not noticed that four months had passed since my last menstrual cycle. With all the symptoms I was feeling, plus confirming the last day I had my period, I had no alternative but to tell Chapi to take me to get a pregnancy test. We had decided that we would go the next day after I got out of school.

I remember that when the school's departure bell rang, Chapi was already waiting for me in his car in front of the gate. When we arrived at the lab and they finished getting my blood, they told me that the results would be ready the following day. The next day we did the same. I got into his car and went to find Adriana, whom we had already told her about everything that was happening. The lab was about five minutes away from Adriana's house. I will never forget that drive to the lab. It was the longest five minutes of my life. There was an incredible silence. When we arrived, Adri and Chapi stayed in the car. I went in to get the blood results, which changed our lives forever. When I walked out of the building, I felt like nothing was around me; I felt like everything was crashing down. I got in the car and just sat there crying. I was scared to think about how I would tell my mom. At that moment, Adri did not help me much because her first words were, "You are screwed with mom." Obviously, it was an automatic reaction on how she felt since she had lived a similar experience when she became pregnant at the age of eighteen.

She realized that her comment made me cry more and she tried to fix it by telling me not to worry, that everything was going to be fine. She told Chapi quietly that he was also screwed when mom found out. We both decided that I would tell mom first. I remember being dropped off at her apartment, I walked in and there was no one. When mom arrived, she quickly realized that something was not right because she saw my face swollen due to all the crying. When I started telling her, she went to her room crying and groaning from the pain she felt. I remember I heard her crying while saying, "Why her? Why me?" Amid her pain and despair, she yelled at me and demanded that I had an abortion. During my crying and pain, I told her that I was so sorry, but I was not going to do that. She did not say anything; she just grabbed her car keys and left. I remember seeing my little sister Liani in her room painting. I felt so embarrassed to know that I had not been able to be a role model for her as a big sister.

A little while later mom returned. She had gone to look for Chapi because she wanted to talk to him. Chapi later told me that he was washing his car outside in the street in front of his house when he saw from afar that mom was coming at full speed. He knew at that time that she already knew what was going on. Mom saw him and told him she wanted to see him at her house in five minutes because they had to talk.

When Chapi arrived at the apartment, my mom had calmed down a little. He came in and sat beside me. He let mom talk and vent. One of the things she asked him first was what he intended to do. He answered that he wanted to marry me. Those were the only words Chapi said all night. My mom insulted him very strongly; she told him many things out of anger, but something I always admired about him at that time was that he never talked back to her, nor was he trying to defend himself. He always kept his head down as a sign of respect and understood the anger she was feeling at that time. After she told us all she had to say, she asked him to leave. Before he left, she told him she was not going to give us the signature required so that we could get married; that she would never allow it (in Puerto Rico, the law allows a child under the age of eighteen to marry when their parents or guardians give them authorization through a signature, through emancipation). He just looked at her and closed the door. From that day on, I stayed at my mom's house.

Days later when she calmed down, we sat down to talk, only her and I. She said that I needed to get an abortion, and I replied again that both Chapi and I made the decision to have the baby. She replied that I had to leave the house and that she was not going to give me the signature so I can get married because she was not going to be part of my failure. At that moment she thought we were not going to last long together. She did not want me to throw it in her face as to why she had allowed me to get married so young. After that conversation, I picked up all my belongings and went to live with Chapi at his parents' house.

THE CIRCUMSTANCES DO NOT DETERMINE YOUR DESTINY

We have all gone through situations where we think we will never get out. Situations that change the course of our future that were full of color and now, everything looks dark and without hope. Everything can change from day to night. Whether it be because of our actions or for the actions of others or even from expected or unexpected events. The reality is that our lives changed.

We are now in an open and deserted field where the only thing we can see is two paths. These paths will take us through two different destinations. One of them looks longer and bumpier than the other. The reality is that the other, although it looks shorter and more attractive, is the path that takes us away from God. When we choose the path God offers us, even if it is full of obstacles and problems, even if it is endless, it guarantees that in the end, we will finish the race better than how we started it.

Whatever you read may seem the opposite of what you normally think. You might ask yourself, "How does path that looks so difficult to walk, be better than one that looks easy?" and you are right. When we choose the way God shows us, He does not guarantee that there will be no problems, but He does guarantee that we will learn from it. Some of the problems may even be the people we will find ourselves on the journey with, who will try to divert and confuse us. They will try to be like mirages; they will imitate an oasis. Problems help us develop resistance and expand knowledge to create new alternatives and become successful at the end of the road. It is okay to get tired during the journey; it is ok to sit and rest, only if it is to recharge our energy and keep walking.

That is where many of us fail. Many times, we prefer to stop halfway and give up because we think we will not achieve it. In this moment I tell you, do not give up! After you breathe deeply and have refreshed yourself in the oasis of God's Word, rise and continue. I promise you that it will be worth getting to the end. God awaits you with the best prize. In the end you will see that you have matured and are no longer the same as when you started. Now you are ready to run your next race.

"Do you not know that in a race all the runners run, but only one gets the prize? Run in such a way as to get the prize. Everyone who competes in the games goes into strict training. They do it to get a crown that will not last, but we do it to get a crown that will last forever.
Therefore I do not run like someone running aimlessly; I do not fight like a boxer beating the air. No, I strike a blow to my body and make it my slave so that after I have preached to others, I myself will not be disqualified for the prize."
(1 Corinthians 9:24-27 NIV)

CHAPTER 12

Forced to be an adult

A nd that was how our stories changed forever. Now we were two young adults who would become parents very soon. It was not easy to have to face the embarrassment in the church either, so we decided to stop attending at that time. We spoke to our youth pastor and the senior pastor, who surprised us with their immense support and love. It was then that we learned the beautiful lesson of having the backs of our neighbors in love. I remember that when we were sharing our decision to leave the church because of the shame we felt, we were told that they would protect us and cover us as God did. The Sunday following that conversation, the senior pastor (our beloved Jr. Vélez), stood us in front of the congregation and shared our situation. When he finished explaining the concern, we had about being judged, he stood in authority and began to speak a message of hope, forgiveness, love, and redemption. He let the congregation know that he did not want anyone rejecting us or speaking bad about us because if so, he would personally take care of those individuals. We will never forget that day. We experienced God's love and protection through our pastors. Because of that and many other things, those pastors will always hold a special place in our hearts.

When we found out about our pregnancy, I was already four months pregnant. The time went by super-fast. As soon as we found out, it was like waking up with all the symptoms of a "stomach virus". I spent my first six months with nausea, vomiting, and dizziness. I even fainted one day. I remember that I was throwing the trash away at Adriana's house when I suddenly lost consciousness and fell over a metal trash can where my head bounced off the edge, hitting my upper lip.

After the accident, Chapi arrived very quickly. Adriana had called him and when he saw me, he was very scared and worried. He had realized that his responsibilities and priorities had changed overnight. How difficult of a time was that, especially, learning to adapt to a life full of responsibilities. This process was tough. I continued to attend school without anyone knowing I was pregnant. I tried to keep the secret as much as I could, but my stomach was quick to show. I remember we used to wear skirt and vest uniforms. It got to the point where I had to keep the button and the zipper of the skirt undone so that it did not squeeze my belly. I kept my vest closed to try to disguise a little, but as time passed, I could not hide my new reality anymore.

I spoke with mom so she could help me talk to the school principal so that I could finish high school. I was at the end of the eleventh grade and wanted to graduate the following year with my friends, with whom I had been friends with since kindergarten. I suffered so much... My bad decisions led me to leave behind a life that I loved and enjoyed, but one that I never valued enough because of things I thought were my priorities at that time.

I knew that the odds of being allowed to stay were minimal, due to the strict rules that the archdiocese required of the Catholic school. I remember that the principal cared for me a lot, as it was almost twelve years that she saw me grow and develop into a young woman. I was one of her favorite students. Even though I gave her "a lot of headaches" (sometimes I pulled pranks), I always stood out in everything I did.

Mom managed to get a private meeting with her, but she told me that I would have to convince the principal. She told me I was the one who got into this mess and now, I should have the responsibility to solve **it. It can sound a little harsh or you can even think that she was a little insensitive on her part, but today I thank her for acting like this; for she taught me to create an awareness of my actions. She taught me that everything we do brings consequences. If we do good things, the consequences will be good, but if we do bad things, the consequences will be bad. That was the key motto in my home since we started our family. To this day it still is, and I remind it daily to my two oldest children, who have now started their own families. My desires and hope are that they will understand that although mom and dad will always be there to help them, their actions will bring consequences that will change their stories for the rest of their lives.**

When I finished presenting my proposal to the principal and my immense desire to graduate with my friends in my alma mater, her answer was that if it were for her, she would accept without hesitation because she knew my heart. The problem was trying to convince her leaders. She suggested to me to go to the offices of the archdiocese and talk to the archbishop and present my concerns to him in the same way. My mom drove me to the office, and I presented myself to the leadership and board members with my heart in my hands. I remember even crying, but nothing I said or did altered his way of thinking. He was noticeably clear and firm in his position and in the laws established in the Catholic Church in relation to situations such as mine. So, they made the decision to get me out of school. That was one of the most painful experiences I had to face in my new reality.

My days of enjoying the surprises that life brought me, a new dawn without responsibility, had been left behind. Living a life where my biggest concerns were what clothes I would wear or how I would fix my hair faded away like magic. Now we had begun, in a forced way, a life as adults.

HOW TO ENJOY A HEALTHY ADOLESCENCE?

One of the advantages of being parents as adolescents is that when our children become teenagers, their youth is not so distant from ours. It is easier to understand and remember those feelings that we all experienced during those years.

How can we forget that adrenaline of every adventure and every challenge we faced? Not to mention the uncontrollable emotions when we saw that special person pass by the inexhaustible laughter among friends.

These are some of the many things every teenager may experience and never forget.

Many times, as adults we focus on the bad things that happen or can happen during our youth, and we forget to cherish those wonderful moments that made us who we are today.

My children can testify that we are parents who understand their concerns and have given them the freedoms necessary to enjoy their youth. Their own friends have often called us the "super cool" parents. We have understood that there is a time for everything and that our best weapon to combat a separation in our relationship is communication and understanding. It is learning not only to speak, but to listen.

It is also important that you understand that any decision you make will bring consequences, whether bad or good. I want you to know that doing the right thing does not mean doing "boring" things; especially if you serve God or want to live as He commands.

Living a life in Christ can be equally or more fun than a life without Him. It is a matter of perspective. When you think that only the bad or prohibited things, either by earthly law or divine law, are the most exciting, then that is when you lose the essence of what is fun.

Doing the wrong thing produces temporary satisfaction and its result will always hurt us in the short or long term. Jesus was a fun man who liked adrenaline. We can see it when He went fishing with his friends, the disciples; when He challenged and calmed the storms; when He preached among multitudes; when He challenged the Pharisees; when He cast out demons; when He talked to the children, when He built things with wood. In short, Jesus knew how to have fun, even being the Son of God.

The fun and adrenaline of a game is in the competition of the teams; this game represents your life. You decide which team to be on. You play on the team that is in favor of your life or you play on the team that is against it. Play clean and choose the winning team, where the coach is Jesus.

"Whoever has ears, let them hear. 'To what can I compare this generation? They are like children sitting in the marketplaces and calling out to others: 'We played the pipe for you,and you did not dance; we sang a dirge, and you did not mourn.' For John came neither eating nor drinking, and they say, 'He has a demon.' The Son of Man came eating and drinking, and they say, 'Here is a glutton and a drunkard, a friend of tax collectors and sinners.' But wisdom is proved right by her deeds."
(Matthew 11: 15-19 NIV)

CHAPTER 13

The Pregnant Girl in High School

I enrolled in a public school to complete my eleventh-grade year. It was very difficult to accept this change. I felt alone in school. Now, I was part of the club of pregnant girls who everyone watched walking in the hallways as we went from one classroom to another. I felt judged and marginalized. I managed to make very few friends because I felt embarrassed and did not have the courage to talk to anyone. To top it off, my nausea and other 'pregnancy' symptoms did not help me concentrate on my classes. Because of this, I went from being an honor roll student to one who struggled with even getting a "C." It was very frustrating, and I felt very lonely. My only refuge was to know that I had Chapi, but he did not talk much about it because he thought he would not understand me, as he also had dropped out of school. I managed to finish eleventh grade by the mercy of God. I thought that my "bad grades" would continue to add to my list of embarrassments.

By that time, I was about to give birth. We lived in my mother-in-law's house for almost two months. During the time that I lived with them, I could see God's care and love through my beloved mother-in-law. She made this stage of my pregnancy easier. I remember she tried to please me in all my cravings, and she would not let me do anything in fear that something would happen to my baby. She always treated me with love and was always looking out for me. That made our relationship grow. I have never had an argument with my mother-in-law and God knows I would do anything for her. I love her with all my heart and will be eternally grateful to her.

It was not easy for Chapi either. He had worked occasionally to earn "a couple bucks" to get some gas to go to the beach or eat…those days were now left behind. He now worked to support his new family. His days of freedom and of living an easy life were over. Now he had to push hard and work hard to bring food to the table and pay rent. His hobby of cars had now moved to second place. Now the money was accounted for and many times it was not enough to survive. We had to apply for all the government assistance that was available to us.

We were able to rent our first apartment; it was small, but it was our new home, our nest of love. We barely had anything. We slept on a sofa bed that I brought from my room when I lived with mom. I remember it was uncomfortable and the mattress rested on a base of metal tubes. Every time we got up, we had marks of the tubes on our backs because of how thin it was, but at least we both fit on it. We did not have a dresser to put our clothes in either. So, we improvised and made one with cardboard boxes. The sofa in the living room was one that had been gifted to us, but that we had to share with cockroaches as we realized it was infested. We were trying to get them out for some time. Conquering the couch was a prolonged battle, but we managed to get the victory... ha, ha, ha. It was in that apartment complex that we met our neighbors that lived behind us, who later became our good friends. They were also newlyweds and were expecting their first born. We had many things in common and we supported each other in this forced process of becoming adults. They played an especially significant role at the stage we were living in. They made our days more pleasant and easy going. I will never forget our long nights of laughter and anecdotes. We were there to welcome their baby girl to their apartment in her mother's arms. Thanks to the birth of their child, I was able to practice many things that I would have to do when it was my turn to bring my little girl home. My friend and I shed many tears together. We will be forever grateful to God for allowing us to meet and grow with them in the time we did, as God knew we needed this so much. They will always be friends that we will treasure.

I remember the first groceries Chapi bought. He bought so many things that most of it spoiled in the fridge. He even bought microwavable food-we did not even have a microwave. We had to ask our friends and neighbors to lend us their microwave so we could eat these foods

Nearing the time to give birth, we were able to buy a crib and a set of sheets for the baby. I already had the hospital bag prepared with everything that had been given to us at the baby shower that my friends from school planned out. I remember going to the stores and looking at the set of clothes, shoes, and sheets that I wanted to bring our baby girl home from the hospital with. They were hand-made with cheesecloth fabric. They were expensive, at least for us it was. I came home crying because I wanted to buy one for our baby and I could not afford it. I spoke to my mom to see if she could purchase the outfit and she did. I still remember how beautiful it was and the excitement of having it. I used to open the box every day to look at it and touch it. I imagined our baby girl with those beautiful little clothes on. The love for our daughter had grown greatly. She became our reason and our motivation for fighting in this difficult life. She represented our hope.

One morning, while we were asleep, I started to feel some strong contractions. When I tried to get up from the bed to go to the bathroom, my water broke. Chapi became nervous and so did I. Because we were both so nervous, we forgot to take the bag that I had prepared for the hospital. Chapi took me to a small hospital nearby, where they were only attending to emergencies. From there, I was taken by ambulance to another hospital.

On June third, 1997, at 1:30 p.m. weighing seven pounds and measuring twenty and a half inches, we received our first blessing. Although she arrived without being planned, we witnessed the birth of the product of our love. Our canelita (how we like to call her, which translates to little cinnamon), our brown sugar; our beautiful Chanía was born.

PREGNANCY IN ADOLESCENCE
One of the most difficult tests I've ever had in my life was to become such a young mother. Although my three children, whom I love with all my strength, are my greatest blessing and pride, I confess that if I could go back in time, my decisions would have been different. I would

have had them under different circumstances.

My life changed rapidly causing many mental injuries that I had to fight with for a long time. The responsibilities that were designed to be assumed in an adult stage hit us and moved us abruptly toward a new life, to which we were not accustomed or ready for. Managing money, debts, the concern of a place to live, and what we would eat was added to the list of responsibilities that two young people had to fulfill.

When I can advise teens who are going through situations like those we lived, I try to stress to them the importance of completing their studies. Academic preparation is one that benefits both parents and the baby on the way; it helps us to have a more stable future.

I stress the importance of being responsible for the upbringing and care of our children and not leave this for the grandparents, uncles/aunts, or any other family members who can help. While support and assistance are much needed to fulfill all the responsibilities that must be dealt with during this process, it does not mean that the responsibility for the upbringing of our kids is going to go to the backburner. On the contrary, the needs of our children must be the priority and that means our time and our main attention is to them. Trust me, it can be done. The most important thing you can give to your child are not materialistic things, but your attention. It is the satisfaction of listening to them say when they are older, "My parents were always there for me. We were their priority."

We had the blessing of raising our children together; this lessened the burden. We both made the decision that I would stay at home raising the children during their younger years, while he worked and provided for the family. I know that everyone does not have this privilege, especially when they are single parents, but I also firmly believe that a balance can be created between time and priorities. The best thing God has done is give us another day. Remember that what you have not accomplished today, you could always do it tomorrow.

The greatest inheritance you can leave your kids is the time and love with which you instruct them. Children are a gift from God, no matter the circumstances in how they were conceived. That little person can be the joy you have always needed in your life. Give it a chance to live.

"Children are a heritage from the Lord, offspring a reward from him. Like arrows in the hands of a warrior are children born in one's youth. Blessed is the man whose quiver is full of them. They will not be put to shame when they contend with their opponents in court." (Psalms 127:3-5 NIV)

CHAPTER 14

My New Family

I gave birth at a hospital that did not have a particularly good reputation but that was where we had our daughter. I had to give birth without any support from my family. They were not able to accompany me in the room. It was a short, but very painful birth. I screamed out of pain and fear in not knowing how to handle the process. The nurses were annoyed with me and yelled at me to shut up. One of them even covered my mouth at one time. But God gave me strength and I was able to have my baby girl naturally without an epidural. This was not because I did not want it, but because they never offered it to me. They just gave me some medication to relieve the pain, but that did not work. It was a very difficult experience for me, physically and emotionally.

When our daughter was born, they put her on my chest and quickly removed her and took her away, making me cry a lot because I could not have her in my arms. When I was finally taken to a room, I asked one of the nurses when I could see my baby. She told me that if I wanted to see her, I had to walk to where all the newborn babies were. I asked her to please tell my boyfriend to bring me the bag we had prepared for the hospital. Thank God she had compassion; she did as I requested and went to tell him. I was wearing the paper gown offered by the hospital all that time. I managed to cover my back with an extra sheet that I found on the bed and went to find my baby.

I walked very slowly because I still felt a little weak and I was exhausted from all the hours I was in labor. Still, nothing stopped me from seeing my daughter. When I asked to enter the room to see her, I was directed to my baby who was wrapped in paper sheets. I will never forget that image when I saw her…I began to cry. My daughter was the only baby who did not cry or sleep. She had her eyes wide open looking around, as if she was looking for something or someone. She was very calm and had her small little hand in her mouth that she was able to pull out of the sheets of paper in which she was wrapped. I grabbed her in my arms and as I cried, I said to her, "Hello my love, Mom is here. You are not alone anymore; I am here to take care of you and protect you." In that moment I experienced my first feeling as a protective mother. The embarrassment and the feeling of being alone disappeared immediately when I had her in my arms. Now I knew that my daughter depended solely and exclusively on me. I stayed there with my daughter in my arms. I kissed her and brought her close to my face so that I could smell her baby scent. I spoke to her and declared words of prosperity and victory over her. I prophesied over her life words of blessings. I promised her that both Mom and Dad would take her hand to help her achieve her purpose in God; that we would always take care of her and protect her. We would teach her about God and His wonderful love so that one day she could have a personal encounter with Him. I promised her that we would never leave her alone and that we would always be there to help her and love her over all things. The next day we were discharged from the hospital, and we were anxious about leaving. I remember seeing Chapi load the car seat. He walked very slowly, preventing any movement from waking or hurting her. He drove toward our apartment super slow. I could not believe that this was the same guy who almost a year ago competed in a clandestine manner with any car that would stand next to him. His interests had changed, and his priorities were now different. He became a dad.

We arrived at our nest, where our beloved friends and neighbors welcomed us. They had some surprises ready that filled my heart. We opened the door to the apartment and when we walked in, we felt very weird. We got everything situated and then pulled her out of the car seat. I held her in my arms and did not want to let her go. We looked at her and kissed her constantly. We told her we loved her repeatedly. We finally put her in her crib. We kept looking at her and thanking God for her. We hugged each other and Chapi, looking at me said, "We did it my love. We are now a family."

THE IMPORTANCE OF FAMILY
In the previous chapter I told you that children are a gift from God and that it is extremely important to devote time and attention to them. I want to stay on that topic, but this time, emphasizing how God thinks about the family and the duties that come with this.

As we look at *Deuteronomy 6:6-9 (NIV)* it says, *"These commandments that I give you today are to be on your hearts. Impress them on your children. Talk about them when you sit at home and when you walk along the road, when you lie down and when you get up. Tie them as symbols on your hands and bind them on your foreheads. Write them on the doorframes of your houses and on your gates."*

Pay attention as the verse begins. God begins with a teaching aimed towards parents as individuals. God exhorts us to have an intimate relationship with Him first. Why do you think He starts by giving us that guideline first? For we cannot give, nor teach, what we do not know. It is so important that you understand that your relationship with God not only benefits you, but also affects everyone around you. When we understand God's love, it is easier to practice and imitate Him. Deciding to love God over everything is a rewarding, yet sacrificial, lifestyle. This means that, like Him, we will die to ourselves to put others before ourselves.

He then exhorts us to commit ourselves to following His commandments. The compromise is a pact, a contract that must not be broken. Doing so brings consequences that will affect us all. Commitment goes beyond emotions; it is a decision on what is good or bad. He then tells us that the commitment we make to Him must be transferred to our children. It makes us responsible for teaching and guiding them while modeling what we learn in their presence. It emphasizes the importance of always making teaching our highest priority, regardless of time and place.

Every family goes through their difficult times, but when God is the center of the home, our burdens will always be easier, and our questions will always be answered. Sometimes that answer is not what we want to hear. So, if you have not made God the center of your family, I urge you to start today. It does not matter the size of your family or your role. God will give you the exact way to practice His commandments in your home. Go ahead, I know you can do it!

CHAPTER 15

First Year of Marriage

I can tell you that the first year was one full of challenges and a lot of learning as new parents, but especially as young parents. We made many mistakes, most of which we laughed at. Seeing Chapi change diapers was hilarious. You can imagine the nausea it gave him, but despite all the challenges, we were always together. We learned, grew, and matured together. The love we had for each other had helped us overcome any obstacle that came our way; especially that new love that our daughter brought out of us. We never thought we could love that much, and our daughter reminded us of that day by day.

I remember Chapi arriving from work and our daughter woke up. He heard her crying and he felt bad. I asked him to pick her up for a moment because I was finishing dinner. He picked her up and while he wasrocking her, the baby kept crying. He got so anxious that he took her to the kitchen so I could feed her, as she cried because she was hungry.

When I finished feeding her, she fell asleep. I went to the bathroom as Chapi was showering. I was going to ask if he wanted me to serve him food but when I opened the shower curtain, I saw him crying. I got scared and asked him what was going on. He replied that he was incredibly sad to see our baby girl cry. I could not hold in my laughter; I started laughing and he closed the curtain fast. He asked me to leave as he laughed from embarrassment and being annoyed with me since I was laughing at him.

In 1998 we decided to get married. I was turning eighteen years old and would be of legal age. We would no longer need my mom's signature to finally get married. We started planning the wedding, but it was very difficult because of our financial situation. The rings we bought were not the rings we wanted, but they were what we could afford. For us, the rings were not that important, but the fact that we could get married was.

During this time, we were going to church, and we felt guilty because we lived together prior to getting married. The only setback was the date of the wedding. It was a month before my eighteenth birthday. We decided to talk to my mom, who agreed to sign the papers and allowed us to get married. By this time, she was calm about our situation. Chapi was winning her over, but she was in love with her new granddaughter, who had changed her life and way of thinking.

Today my mom loves Chapi to the extent that most of the time she defends him more than me. They have managed to develop a beautiful relationship. My mom does not miss a single opportunity to praise him and let him know how grateful she is that he has remained by my side. I managed to finish my fourth year of high school by exam or also known as the General Equivalency Diploma (GED). My new role as a mother consumed most of my time and I could not return to school. I made my daughter my priority and understood that the best decision for our family was that I was going to take care of her while Chapi provided.

I thank God so much that I had the privilege of having a man, who from the first day that he knew that he was going to be a father, stayed by my side. Even though he knew it was not going to be easy for him, he gave us the blessing of staying home. He understood that his new duty was to provide everything necessary to live. He understood that his role of loving and protecting his family was above everything. He loved us unconditionally and that gave him strength to go to work every day.

We enjoyed that first year with our baby so much! She has always been so easy to raise; she was a good baby. Wherever we went, she was there, including when we went to the beach…the only place my husband was not able to give up. Surfing was his passion and he used to do it every day, but now he shared his hobbies with his family. I tried to surf with him once when we were dating, but I could not do it like him. Chapi had a lot of talent in that sport. I used to love to sit and watch him do his tricks; his love for surfing showed through his talent. I was his number one fan.

BECOME YOUR HUSBAND'S #1 FAN

It is necessary that us women honor our husbands or partners and become their "number one fans." Society has always stipulated that only women should be honored and praised for their work and/or everything we do. I understand that this has had a lot to do with the history and trajectory that women have had to live to be recognized, but when the balance is lost, the purpose is lost. We cannot punish everyone for the mistakes of a group. There are still good men who love and fight to maintain an untroubled home. The world is full of working, loving, faithful, family-oriented men and the list goes on... For this reason, they deserve to be recognized and celebrated daily. My husband is a living example of one of them. He may not be perfect, but fights day by day to make us happy. Bravo to men like him who take their position as priests of the home.

"Submit to one another out of reverence for Christ. Wives, submit yourselves to your own husbands as you do to the Lord. For the husband is the head of the wife as Christ is the head of the church, his body, of which he is the Savior." (Ephesians 5: 21-23 NIV)

CHAPTER 16

Our Family Keeps Growing

W e moved to a better apartment near my mom's house; so close, we were neighbors! The apartment had one bedroom. I think the size was not even eight hundred square feet. We were able to change our sofa bed to an actual bed with a metal base. We also managed to change our improvised cardboard dresser. Our new dresser was given to us and restored to our liking. The love of doing construction and renovation projects in our home started around the year 2000. We enjoyed seeing things that were useless become things that would draw the attention of everyone who saw it. It was that same year that my husband discovered the incredible talent he had in construction and engineering. He realized that all those years of working on wood with his dad and older brother was worth it

I remember that our first large renovation project in our home was a small wooden wall that Chapi built in the apartment. This wall divided the tiny kitchen from our tiny living room. I describe it as tiny because like I said that apartment was exceedingly small. It looked so pretty when it was finished. The wall was built so well that the apartment owner could not believe this young man had the ability to create something like that.

The woman that owned the apartments we lived in saw me grow up. She was the mother of one of my best friends at school. It was a blessing to move there. She was always looking out for my family; she even cared for Chapi a lot. I remember that she always told me that he was a "good boy" and that I hit the lottery with him. Even though we were so blessed and happy with our new life, it was a little difficult for me to live there because I saw when my friend was going out or was getting picked up by the girls from school to hangout. Many times, they invited me, but I would decline because I preferred to stay with my daughter. I never liked leaving her under the care of anyone. So, I watched them leave as they laughed and enjoyed their youth, without having to worry about adult responsibilities. As they left, I would think to myself "Wow, that could be me."

Seeing my little girl grow up made this feeling of sadness disappear. She was so sweet and loving. She always wanted to help me, followed me everywhere, and talked a lot...ha, ha, ha. We saw her play alone in the house and we began desiring to have another baby. At the end of that same year, we planned to have another child. To our surprise, two weeks later we knew that our desires had been fulfilled.

Even though I was also experiencing bad pregnancy symptoms at the beginning of that pregnancy, it was not as strong as the one I went through with Chanía. We were able to enjoy the second pregnancy more. When we learned that we were going to have a boy, we were filled with joy; it was going to be a completely new experience. Planning a change to a lifestyle that we had grown used to while raising a girl was an adventure. My daughter was almost three years old and like us, she could not wait to meet the newest member of our family. On April fifteenth, 2000, we received our second blessing, our boy, our beloved Adriel.

Our delivery experience on this second occasion was completely different. We had Adriel in a private hospital where we were treated with care from the moment we arrived there. They even allowed Chapi to be with me during the delivery, but he did not get there on time. I remember that when I was close to being ten centimeters dilated, he decided to go eat at the hospital cafeteria. Oh, the nerve of him that he had to do so at that moment. When he came back to the room, he was greeted by his son who was in my arms and his wife, whose face was full of disappointment and anger. I could not believe that during the last minute he got hungry. Now, every time we remember and tell our children the story, we laugh.

We were now a family of four in a one-bedroom apartment where we all slept together. The experience of having a boy was beautiful; it was like starting everything again for the first time. Chanía wanted to help me with everything. She was excited to have a baby at home.

Since a youthful age, Adriel has always liked cars and any means of transportation that can be used in races, just like his father. Even to this day, this is still one of the passions he shares with his dad.

Adriel was so cheerful, always smiling at everyone, especially his older sister who was always trying to play with him. He is still the clown of the family. He continues to make us all laugh with his unexpected conversations and his crazy and unique pranks. I loved seeing my children grow up and how each day they were full of surprises from their jokes and pranks. I still enjoy it to this day, even now with them being adults.

HIDDEN TALENTS

Who would have thought that a twenty-two-year-old man, who only lived for the beach and on the beach, would discover and develop a talent for woodworking? A talent that he always possessed and did not even know it. Financial prosperity was seen in our home through the talent that God gave Chapi.

Many times, God surprises us with talents that we did not know we possess through unexpected situations. How good does this feel? It is a feeling of satisfaction and feeling important in some way. This feeling of being able to do something for ourselves can often feel like we won the lottery.

It is not a terrible thing to be proud of everything we have accomplished through hard work and effort. The problem is when pride becomes arrogance. When we forget who the root is and focus on the fruit, the fruit becomes bitter, and its flavor is damaged. Arrogance is a worm that eats the root little by little, until it kills the plant completely. Never forget to honor God in all that you achieve. Everything we achieve is through His mercy and grace; just as we receive it, it can also be taken away from us.

"AND SAID:
'NAKED I CAME FROM MY MOTHER'S WOMB,
AND NAKED I WILL DEPART. THE LORD GAVE
AND THE LORD HAS TAKEN AWAY; MAY THE
NAME OF THE LORD BE PRAISED.' IN ALL THIS,
JOB DID NOT SIN BY CHARGING GOD WITH
WRONGDOING." (JOB 1:21-22 NIV)

CHAPTER 17

Very Busy Raising Our Kids

We were growing financially as we managed to acquire more customers in our carpentry business. "My Negrito," as I usually call him out of love, worked day and night to provide what was needed for us. The years of surfing and going to the beach had been forgotten. My role as a housewife was exhausting. I now had two children under the age of five running and playing everywhere.

Adriel was highly active since he was young. I had to give him my full attention because I did not know which tree, kitchen furniture, or anything else he would potentially climb on. His favorite game was to hide from Mom and Dad. One day we were in El Morro, a historic place in Puerto Rico with a large grass pasture, spending the day flying kites or "chiringas," as Puerto Ricans call them. I remember that while looking for something to eat in the cooler we had brought, Adriel disappeared in the middle of the crowd. The park was quite busy. We were close to a very deep slope, which I was overly cautious about not letting my children nearby. When I realized that Adriel was not with us, I began to ask everyone if they had seen my boy. My mind began to think of the worst; I thought he had fallen down the cliff or even that he had been kidnapped. In short, the worst thoughts became present right in that moment. After about 10 minutes of searching for him, my nerves got the best of me. I began to cry and scream that I had lost my child. We began to pray as we looked for him and suddenly, the person we thought was not going to find him because of her vision, saw him in the distance. Adriana began shouting, "Look there!" When we saw him, he was near the door of the castle of El Morro. It was about 100 to 200 feet away. I ran to get him. When I got to where he was, I started crying even harder. I hugged him and kissed him without letting him go, while I thanked God for that miracle.

MIRACLES STILL HAPPEN

How many times do we miss the miracles that God gives us daily? This could have happened to anyone for reasons that cannot be avoided; it would be another story to tell, but the beauty of having a relationship with God is that He uses events like this throughout our lives to teach us a lesson and make Himself present.

We need to learn how to find God in the smallest and finest details of our lives and give gratitude to each life lesson that helps us grow and learn every day; let us be conscious and attentive. My sister's vision was not an impediment for her to see what her heart was looking for. Let us look at the world around us with the eyes of the heart and spirit. Do not become blind to the spirit.

"FOR THOUGH WE LIVE IN THE WORLD, WE
DO NOT WAGE WAR AS THE WORLD DOES.
THE WEAPONS WE FIGHT WITH ARE NOT
THE WEAPONS OF THE WORLD. ON THE
CONTRARY, THEY HAVE DIVINE POWER TO
DEMOLISH STRONGHOLDS. WE DEMOLISH
ARGUMENTS AND EVERY PRETENSION
THAT SETS ITSELF UP AGAINST THE
KNOWLEDGE OF GOD, AND WE TAKE
CAPTIVE EVERY THOUGHT TO MAKE IT
OBEDIENT TO CHRIST.
(2 CORINTHIANS 10: 3-5 NIV)

CHAPTER 18

The Trunk of Prosperity and Forgetfulness

We moved from the city to the countryside. God prospered us to the point that we managed to begin building our own house without a loan. We were able, for the first time in our marriage, to give Christmas gifts not only to our children, but to our entire family. That Christmas was an immense joy and we thanked God for what he had done with us.

We began the construction of a two-bedroom house on land that we had graciously inherited from my dad in the town of Morovis, Puerto Rico. We were not able to build a garage, or even a driveway that would reach our home, but it was still our home, and we did not owe it to anyone.

Later we were able to expand our home to four bedrooms with three and a half bathrooms and a four-car garage. We built a huge workshop for Chapi's woodworking at the bottom of the hill where the land ended but still remarkably close to the house. It was a prolonged process and full of obstacles, but it was well worth it.

There were also years of many challenges in our marriage since we had grown and matured more. We were no longer in the "honeymoon stage." We were now adults with responsibilities as a family, but also as individuals. We used to argue every time we started a project in the house because we started it and never finished it. I believe it was around this time that God began with our transformation. I remember that I would often fight with Chapi because he would spend most of his free time on his new hobby of remote-control cars or remote-control helicopters. I was annoyed that he would often spend hours playing with his toys instead of finishing the projects we left incomplete. He would also leave every weekend for car races. I went with him at first, but then I stopped going because I did not like the atmosphere. In addition, I saw that this hobby had brought separation between us. We argued a lot and failed to compromise.

Despite those arguments, we managed to reconcile ourselves, but made the mistake of avoiding the cause of the problems and ignoring our differences. We began to put our feelings aside. We created a trunk of forgetfulness to the point where we would avoid confrontation thinking it would go away. What a big mistake!

THE IMPORTANCE OF CREATING A BALANCE

It is different now. We have been able to find a balance and respect our time apart from each other; something that is necessary to grow as individuals but allows us to grow as a couple as well. I love seeing him enjoy his hobbies and then sharing with me his experiences, triumphs, or really anything that happened during his alone time.

Chapi has always been a man who, at the time of an argument, tries not to speak to avoid problems and anger. I, on the other hand, like to say what is on my mind at that moment. I have been characterized by having a very explosive personality by expressing my emotions in an incredibly open way and by using a tone of voice that is too loud and aggressive. My sisters and mom used to call me "The fighter."

I put that in the past because God has transformed my character and today, I am a different person; my old character brought me a lot of problems. Sometimes it is better to remain quiet in the moment than to speak at the wrong moment. That has been something that has cost me a lot. I had to learn and understand this the hard way. I am still working with many areas of my character today. I have improved a lot, but I know I still have a lot to change. I will accomplish this in my lifetime and in my walk with God. I have learned to rest my problems in Him, and I understand that this is a process, one that I can only be focused on today.

"I instruct you in the way of wisdom and lead you along straight paths." (Proverbs 4: 11 NIV)

In the next chapter you will learn a little more about me and my family background. You will be able to get a clearer idea of the outcome of my mistakes, my experiences, and how God transformed me.

CHAPTER 19

MY FAMILY HISTORY

I am the second born of three sisters; Adriana, who is five years older than me and my younger sister, Sylvia Liani, who is four years younger than me. Of the three, I was always the one with the strongest character. Adriana was the party animal, Liani was the jokester, and I was the fighter...ha, ha, ha. It sounds funny, but I have been battling with my character for years.

I grew up in a close-knit family; a family full of energy and that was always cheerful. A family where everyone did everything; where the "shy in the parranda (Christmas carolers) stays in the garage" (a quote from a Christmas carol that we use to sing every Christmas). I assure you that it was like that. If you did not join us, you would stay outside, but most of the time, the shy one always ended up joining in because of the joy, love, and

The way my family made you feel included it was magical. Staying up until the break of dawn was normal at parties. As a kid, I grew up sleeping on my friends' couches during Christmas caroling or really any party that my family attended. For us, "Christmas was all year long." I loved being around my mom and her sisters; all of them are so unique and special.

FAMILY ANECDOTES

One of my best childhood memories was one of my birthday parties. I think I was six years old. I remember that Mom and Dad asked my Uncle Frank and my Aunt Isabel to dress up as clowns. That birthday is still vastly remembered today; my family made it unforgettable. They made me feel special, unique, loved… In short, they treated me like only they could.

At that birthday party, there was everything from a night of talent shows with whoever wanted to participate, games, prizes, and even a puppet show. I remember that the puppeteer was Uncle Frank; I liked to go behind the stage that Dad created with cardboard to see him perform. There was also an improvised play by my aunts, their husbands, my mom, and my dad. That play was epic, and I think that is why I love the theater so much. I sat on the terrace floor watching all their performances and the mistakes they made, in which they managed to make them look like part of the drama.

Music has always been in our culture. Every party ended around dawn with my uncles and aunts singing and playing instruments. Even to this day, it remains the same. I have been blessed to have been born and raised around such a talented family. The talents in everyone, from my uncles to my cousins, have always been essential and palpable, but what has truly characterized our family is the love and union we have with each other. My cousins and I had the best childhood because we were to experience the family union. Since I was a little girl, I was able to learn that family is first. The best place to be is with your family. I did not have the privilege of sharing a lot of time with my dad's side of the family, but those in his family I did get to meet, I keep in touch with.

MY CHARACTER

Those who know me know that I am a multifaceted person. I love creativity, arts, nature, and people. Of those four things, the last one was the most difficult for me to learn to love. Yes, I wrote it well; it cost me!

It was very difficult for me to do things in public or to be as sociable as my family used to be. They would act as if they knew a stranger for years and hold endless conversations with them. Of my three sisters, I was always the one who watched them dance. I may have danced a little (remember it is hard to not be contagious when you are with my family), but then I quickly returned to the corner of the sofa. I saw my sisters sing, joke, and dance endlessly and tirelessly, especially my older sister who even to this day, is always the last one dancing at the party. My God, I do not know where she gets so much energy from…ha, ha, ha. In the meantime, I laughed and enjoyed time with them; it was so difficult for me to socialize! I would fight with everyone, even with God. I cried because I hated to be like that. There came a point where I hated myself so much because I could not be like others.

As an adult, married and with children, I began to pour my frustration and anger into the ones I loved the most: my husband and my children. I did a lot of harm to them with my words and many times, I had physically mistreated my two older children. Something I will suffer for the rest of my life. I had always been very eloquent with my words, but at that time, I used them to hurt and harm. Every time I was in the presence of God I wept bitterly with repentance and anger with myself.

ONE DAY AT A TIME

My character led me to make the worst mistakes of my life. My transformation was a lengthy process; it was not like magic that suddenly happened, though God could do it, but the way He did it was little by little. I would like to tell you a story about the day I met God and how all my problems and bad habits disappeared as if it were magic. However, the problems were on the rise, and I would never change the experiences I went through for nothing in the world. This process has made me discover areas in me that I had no knowledge existed and everything has led me to recognize the true meaning of the cross.

Sometimes the pain and concern from these types of processes cloud our eyes, preventing us from seeing it clearly and seeing beyond the problems. We lock ourselves in our suffering, causing us to push away reality and those around us. We create multiple characters that we learn to use with people according to the moment or occasion we are in to prevent our true self from coming to light. But let me tell you something...nothing you can do to try and hide the problem will be worth it.

At the end of the day, you will face your reality and realize that everything remains the same and that emptiness and unhappiness are the reality of the unreal world you have created. The reason I decided to write this book is not just to tell you my life story or to entertain you, but for you to see the transforming power of Jesus' blood. I am not a religious fanatic, although I am His number one fan since He transformed my life and filled it with His undeserved love.

"DO NOT CONFORM TO THE PATTERN OF THIS WORLD, BUT BE TRANSFORMED BY THE RENEWING OF YOUR MIND. THEN YOU WILL BE ABLE TO TEST AND APPROVE WHAT GOD'S WILL IS- HIS GOOD, PLEASING AND PERFECT WILL." (ROMANS 12: 2 NIV)

CHAPTER 20

Birth of Our Third Blessing

At the beginning of 2008 we wanted to have another baby, as we felt that our oldest two were growing extremely fast. We discussed our finances and concluded that we were ready. One month after our conversation, I found out that I was pregnant with our beloved little girl, Guainía Anani, my beautiful water flower that God gave us. Her name is particularly special: Guainía Anani means "territory of a water flower." To choose it, we used the same dictionary of indigenous voices that my parents used to choose my name. Zuanía means "firm land." God showed me my daughter's name in a story I wrote for my children. I would like to share the story with you:

A MYSTERIOUS GIFT

This is the story of a girl and a boy, Little natives who were siblings.
They are raised on the beautiful island where the coquí lives and the painful morivivi grows.
Where the gray kingbird and the parrot fight in the air for who will be the first to eat the rose apple.
The beautiful girl comes up with an idea: she will give her mother something she doesn't expect.

"Heading to the forest we will both go; there we will
search with patience and love."
The boy accompanies her, as his sister trusts that the little
warrior will protect her during the journey.
They undergo the search for a treasure that is still
mysterious; they want it to be something very beautiful.
They cannot imagine it, but they do trust, for God has
given them a little clue.
Heading towards the bush that they keep watching, they
realized they are almost there.
Holding hands, they go excited, smiling as they see a river
God has led them to.
There in the water a light shined.
The little girl, a little scared, says to the warrior "I dare
not, you go."
Not scared and without any fear, the warrior went
confidently walking to find the treasure.
Tucked into the water he observes the area. He sees the
plants that surround the water. There are many flowers
that are different colors, different sizes, and have different
scents.
Amazed at the beauty, he does not realize that in front of
him is the surprise.
In the bright light, there is a huge cocoon. The child,
amazed, watches it proudly.
"Sister, sister, dear sister come and see; we have found
what you have been longing for."

Without thinking twice, she trusts her brother, she desires
to know what has amazed him. Anxiously she walks to
him, although she does not know what it is. The light and
her brother do not let her see it.
When she finally saw the beautiful cocoon, she cried with

joy, for she never imagined what the surprise could be.
God from the Highest asked them:
"Are you ready? The time has come to show you guys the
treasure that I have created for both of you."
The cocoon opens and inside is a beautiful baby girl who
is sleeping.
The boy, curious, asks, "And what will she be named?"
The girl answers, "Ask God, He will tell us."
She represents my purity; in her you will see my beauty.
Beautiful water flower that both of you followed here;
Because of that, you will call her **Guainía Ananí.**

The birth of our baby was a memorable event.
Everyone in the family was amazed with her. From the first
day we knew that she was conceived, to the moment she
was born, she filled us with love for all. I enjoyed that
pregnancy so much. I did not suffer as bad from "stomach
symptoms." My kids loved to feel their little sister move.
Adriel was overly impressed when my belly took unusual
forms; it seemed to him that I had an alien inside me. The
day of having the baby came and everything went
normally. It was painful, but not as much as Adriel's birth.
Instead, this time was fast. I arrived at the hospital at seven
in the morning at three centimeters dilated and had finished
giving birth at noon.

This time Chapi was with me throughout labor. He
was incredibly supportive at all times. I remember the look
he gave me every time I would get a contraction; he
caressed me and told me things to make me feel better. It
was an event that changed Chapi for the rest of his life.
Seeing his wife endure so much pain and bringing another
human to the world was an experience that transformed his

perspective about me. Being a witness to seeing his new addition breathe now in his arms, left him without words. I remember that as I looked at her, he said, "How beautiful is our baby, Zuanía. She has a lot of hair." Even though it sounds funny, I knew what he was trying to tell me. He was experiencing the miracle of love that grows and abounds. Now we were mature and could understand the wonderful love of parents towards children and how it multiplies. We were so happy and excited about this new stage that we had just undertaken; we were now parents of three and loved the idea. My children kept looking at her and caressing her. They kept saying how beautiful and small she was. By that time, Chanía was eleven years old and Adriel eight; both were immensely helpful during the stage when Guaini, as we call her fondly, was an infant. Guainía has always been a very loving and friendly girl; she loves to talk to people and give them love.

A NEW SEASON OF RAISING

In my opinion, I think the reason we were able to enjoy more of this pregnancy and parenting stage of our baby was because we were more mature and emotionally and financially prepared. That is why I use my life testimony to advise others, especially my children, who have already started their own families. We advise them to wait and prepare well. We tell our two oldest children to make the decision to have children when they feel they are stable in their marriage. Although it does not matter the situation in which a child comes from, I am a faithful believer that every person comes to this world for a purpose to be of blessing and transformation, but organization is vital to everything we do in our lives. It gives us a sense of security and trust, but every story is different, and God's grace and mercy are inexplicable. Both Chapi and I are eager to become grandparents and experience that beautiful stage. We are filled with hope every time we think of our grandchildren, who have not yet been born, but whom we love so much without knowing them.

I also believe, based on my own experience, that God allows us to experience certain situations in specific seasons. Every new stage begins with a process of preparation that costs a lot of pain and sacrifice. This happens so that, once wisdom is reached to understand the stage to which God led us to, we can enjoy it more easily and the blessings that come with it, even if we encounter difficulties that will always come in each of our new seasons.

"Blessed is the man who remains steadfast under trial, for when he has stood the test he will receive the crown of life, which God has promised to those who love him."
(James 1: 12 ESV)

CHAPTER 21

Beginning of Our Exodus

T he year 2009 was a very difficult year; one full of many changes and challenges. This was when the economic recession began in Puerto Rico. We began to see the effects on our finances, but above all we began to experience the need for a transformation in our lives, both personally and spiritually. Something in us was different; we could feel it. It was time for a change, but we did not know and could not understand what it was. One day after Chapi was frustrated with work and shared how difficult his day had been, I presented him with the possibility of leaving for the United States. He opened his eyes widely and said to me, "When I was on my way home, I was listening to a preacher on the radio. He prophesied that it was time to go out and that God would take us to distant lands." He told me that when he heard him say that he felt the Holy Spirit unsettle him. He told God in that moment that if what he was feeling was from Him, to let me feel it too.

We did not have in mind the idea of leaving our island and less so when we were in the process of completing the expansions on the house. When Chapi tells me about the experience he had along the way, we both understood that God was talking to us and that we had entered a new stage in our lives.

I cried a lot because although I believed and knew that what we should do was God's command, I did not like the idea of moving to a strange place, where we would have to start from nothing again; where we would have to speak a language that was not ours. We were comfortable in Puerto Rico and that was one of the things I was afraid to give up. I did not want to leave the island, our house, our family, friends, our dreams, in short… leave our entire lives behind. Yet, we believed and obeyed God.

IN OBEDIENCE THERE IS BLESSING

Many times, we pass up new opportunities that God offers us because we are not able to leave our comfort zone. We get used to our daily amenities and routines, making it difficult for us to accept new challenges. How can you learn something new if you do not get the chance to experience new things? God wants us to overcome our fears and to trust in His challenges. He knows what is best for us and if He presents us with a new challenge, He knows that we can achieve it. Today I encourage you to analyze your life and see areas where you can learn new things. Sometimes you put things aside because of the fear of doing them or because you simply do not want to change your routine. God is a creative God and like everything, He teaches us in a different and authentic way. Let us learn to trust Him more and His plans, even though we may not understand them at that particular moment.

"'FOR I KNOW THE PLANS I HAVE FOR
YOU,' DECLARES THE LORD, 'PLANS TO
PROSPER YOU AND NOT TO HARM YOU,
PLANS TO GIVE YOU HOPE AND
FUTURE.'" (JEREMIAH 29:11 NIV)

"'FOR MY THOUGHTS ARE NOT YOUR
THOUGHTS, NEITHER ARE YOUR WAYS MY
WAYS,' DECLARES THE LORD."
(ISAIAH 55:8 NIV)

CHAPTER 22

It is Time to Leave

God closed all financial doors on us; yes, you read that right. God was the one who put pressure on us to understand that it was time for a transformation in our lives. The change of atmosphere did not occur because of the problems we were experiencing; it was not the place we were in, nor the financial situation we were going through, not even the differences we were living through as a marriage.

Both Chapi and I are absolutely certain that God allowed certain inconveniences in our lives so that we could enter a new stage to which He would take us and cause a radical transformation in our lives.

When we finally understood that it was time, we made the tough decision to leave the island and start a new life away from the one we established in Puerto Rico and our home that we had built with so much effort. It was the most difficult decision we have ever made. We felt uneager to leave, scared, and uneasy. Without knowing what was waiting for our future, we still trusted and believed in the word that God had given us as a family.

GOD BEGAN PRUNING IN OUR LIVES

A while ago I finished reading a book that I think is the best book I have read. I loved this book because those who know me, know the love I have toward nature and my passion for plants and cultivation. The book I read and highly recommend you read is called **Chasing Vines** by Beth Moore. In this book the author uses a vine to teach us the different processes that the plant takes to produce the best grapes. In one of the chapters of the book called Pruning, she explains the importance of pruning in plants, but especially in the vine. It makes a comparison and teaches how necessary pruning is for a plant to bear fruit.

According to Beth, it may appear that both for the plant and for the vine viticulturist, who is the person who grows grapes or vines, pruning produces irreparable damage. The author explains in the book that to achieve an excellent harvest for the following season, pruning is necessary.

One of my favorite quotes from the book is, "**God does not prune us all on the same inviolable rule, but every fruitful branch, without exception, will experience cuts. Jesus declared it in John 15:2: ≪God prunes the branches that do bear fruit, so that they may give even more ≫.**"

Beth teaches us that there are moments in our lives when we think we are comfortable, bearing fruits, but the time comes in a vine, in this case our lives, where fruit production stagnates, and a pruning is necessary to stimulate growth and generate a greater production of fruits for the next season that awaits us.

Wow! This was so revealing to my life. How necessary and important it is for God to prune us. Sometimes we think that the losses or negative situations we are going through are synonymous with failure, or the end of our lives, but the reality is that it is not. Sometimes it is our Father's will to allow certain things to help us grow and bear more fruits; I write "sometimes" because there are occasions where the negative things, we go through are the product of bad decisions we make, and those decisions carry consequences.

God is a God of love and all He does is out of love, even if we do not understand the process. At the moment, it may seem unfair and feel like God has abandoned us, but the truth is that our Worker of excellence is pruning us with love so that we can produce more fruit.

"God cuts out a vine that bears fruit just to increase its productivity. That's why growing up can look a lot like shrinking."
-Beth Moore-

CHAPTER 23

Arriving to Texas

By that time, my younger sister Liani and her husband Frank lived in the state of Texas. They had moved there because my Aunt Lucy had offered them to live with her for a while. My sister always liked the idea of living in the United States and took this opportunity my aunt offered her just to experience it, even though Texas was not the state of her preference. Liani and Frank were already living in Texas for almost three years when they offered us to move in with them. My sister and brother-in-law Frank were a blessing to our lives; they welcomed Chapi, who left Puerto Rico first, and he stayed at their home. They helped him out a lot.

Chapi had to learn to adapt to a country where he did not speak the language and where he went from a business owner to a construction employee in demolition. He felt like a slave for the number of hours he worked, the type of work he did, and the pay he received. He was away from us for three months; three months where he suffered physically and emotionally for an involuntary separation. He had to strive to be able to provide for his family. We cried all the time when we spoke, especially when he talked to the kids.

What we did not do when we were dating, we were doing now while married, talking on the phone. We talked for hours and did not get tired. I had never missed him as much as I did during those times. We were desperate to be reunited and the wait seemed endless to us.

Since we started dating, we had never been separated and now we had to experience it abruptly and unintentionally. The goal was for him to stay there for six months to a year to settle financially and then come back and get us. I could not endure this pain, and thanks to Liani, Frank, my aunt Lucy, and her husband Edwin, we managed to come over by surprise. It was a very emotional moment where we all cried. At last, we were all together again!
We lived in my sister's house for a few months, where they welcomed us with openness and love, but we understood that it was time to have our own house.

After Chapi found a permanent job, we made the decision to buy a house. So, we embarked on the new adventure of buying a home for the first time. We were blessed during this journey, and we bought a new house, one recently built; we were so happy! But that achievement could not have been possible without the help of my stepfather Rubén, who helped us buy it.

My mom remarried several years after my dad's death. God allowed me to experience and enjoy the love of a father through Rubén. Even though I no longer lived with Mami when they got married, I was drawn to him as if he were my real dad. My children considered him their grandfather, and Guainía learned to call him "Abuelito" (grandpa) Rubén. My stepfather was a blessing to the whole family, especially my mom. He was a man who we loved, and we will be grateful for everything he did for my mom and for us, his daughters. Unfortunately, in February first 2021, my dad departed to dwell with God. I love you Rubén and miss you every single day. God gave me the best second dad and that is why I want to share a letter I wrote in his honor.

Twenty-six years ago, I had to go through the tragic experience of losing my biological father; my first great love, the great Adrián Gamaliel Molina. The absence of his presence impacted my life.

I was saddened because I knew I would never find a father of the caliber and quality of my dad; Adrián would be hard to replace. Two years passed and to my amazement, a man who would change this thought entered our lives. As always, God exceeded my expectations. He knew that there would never be a replacement, but better yet, he would add what my life needed. He gave me a second dad, my flaquito (skinny), my papito (daddy), Rubén Dario Reyes.

Today, it is my turn to experience for the second time the pain of having to bury my dad's body, but this time I do it with a consciousness that I did not have before. A body is buried, but it lives forever through his teachings, his values, and his joy; the one that always modeled and taught us, his daughters, and all those who had the joy of knowing him. Papito (daddy) of my life, I will miss you all this life, but I rest in the hope that we will reunite again and this time, we will live together for eternity with our Creator. Until soon papito (daddy), my flaquito (skinny), fly high.

KEY PEOPLE IN OUR LIVES

God will always bring people into our lives that will be a blessing. People who will help us through their words and actions. He shows us His infinite love, even with those details of allowing the right people to reach our lives that will impact us in a positive way and that will be part of our history of transformation. Thank you, God, for the people who are part of our lives, whether on a temporary or permanent basis, but those who leave us in a state of gratitude and love, which we will be reminded of them eternally.

CHAPTER 24

Vacations in South Carolina

T he adaptation in Texas was extremely complicated, especially having to get used to a new flora and fauna (plants and animals). One thing that did not help our transition to Texas was that the year we moved there, one of the largest droughts in the state of Texas history happened. As a result, everything was dry and dead. It looked like the old western movies. We could even see the dry tumbleweeds rolling down the road because of the winds, just like in cowboy movies. So, imagine the shock that we felt, especially for me, this jibarita (country girl) from the middle of the mountain of the island, who loved to go out every morning and admire the beautiful colorful scenery that I found in my patio. Our house in Puerto Rico was surrounded by mountains and nature.

Now, the only green we could see was the grass of some neighbors who had their yard painted; a business that I will never understand because to tell you the truth, I do not like it at all. Anyway, it was not easy to get used to a strange country. Otherwise, we did like it, but that specific detail weighed heavily on me to create pressure on Chapi to leave Texas.

In the summer of 2011, we went to visit Adriana and Abraham, who had moved to South Carolina. We fell in love with the flora and fauna of that place; it was beautiful. I remember that they drove us into some mountainous areas, a place that brought me memories of the mountains of Puerto Rico due to the peculiar smell of humid land or "mountain smell," as I like to call it. That is when I let what my natural eyes saw become more important than what my spiritual eyes could see.

So, we thought about moving to North Carolina on the border of both Carolinas. We made the decision to drive for a weeklong stay and vacation at our sibling's home, who lived in the town of Fort Mill, South Carolina. We thought that our desires came from God. We wanted to use that as an excuse for an offer that our siblings had made to help us move there and help them in a ministry they wanted to open. So, we thought that going with them was going to be to our benefit because we were going to be working in the ministry. Oh, but how blind we were...

THE BEAUTY OF THE DESERT

When we think of a desert, the most extreme descriptions come to mind. For example, a dry, desolate place, where temperatures and climate are extreme and impossible to make it your home. But the desert is much more than our eyes can see.

It is an extremely prominent place in our ecosystem. So important, that without them, the cycle of life in many places on Earth are not possible. Deserts are rich in certain minerals that are transported around the world through the intense winds generated by their extreme climates. Many of these minerals are vital to the survival of forests and jungles around the world. So, once again we see how God teaches us through nature that appearances often deceive us. What we think is dry and dead produces life and growth for others.

In those moments of my life, I thought I was going to die in that place that looked dry and ugly. And to think that the most beautiful place my natural eyes were seeing was going to be where I would experience death. Today when I see images of deserts, I cannot help but see their beauty because I now see them from another perspective. You may think that the decisions you make are for a noble cause, but that does not mean that God is in the matter. How important and necessary it is to learn to listen, but above all, to recognize the voice of our Master. Let us tune our spiritual ears and learn to recognize His voice that tells us, "I will make you flourish in the wilderness."

"'My sheep listen to my voice; and I know them, and they follow me. I give them eternal life, and they shall never perish; and no one will snatch them out of my hand.'"
(John 10: 27-28 NIV)

CHAPTER 25

One Bad Decision

As a consequence of not waiting on God and acting out in our despair in the adaptation process in the state of Texas, we made a decision that changed and marked our lives forever. Even though our intentions were good, we decided to leave without consulting with God. We never received confirmation from Him and we still chose to leave. We were discussing whether we were going to be leaving Texas for several months. It was a difficult process, especially for me because I could not understand the idea that first, we had left our land and everything that had cost us so much sacrifice and secondly, we were now in a new country and city where I did not want to be. We were so confused that little by little, we lost our focus.

Despite everything, we had made many friendships and were good financially. One of the biggest reasons I was staying in Texas was my little sister Liani, who by that time was pregnant with my nephew Adrián. I wanted to stay with them and be able to go through that experience of seeing her give birth. Our daughters Guainía and Isabella (Liani's oldest) were growing up together, but the desire to leave was overwhelming. We put our house up for rent and went driving for eighteen hours. Chapi pulled a trailer full of our

123

belongings with his van, while I was driving a van full of more belongings, with our three children and three dogs. Everything was a great crazy adventure. We were incredibly happy and excited about the new stage of life we would start soon. We never imagined that we would be living one of the worst trials we would go through in our marriage. We arrived and settled in Charlotte, North Carolina and lived fifteen minutes from the South Carolina border where our siblings lived. Everything worked out well; we found jobs, rented a house, and started taking root there. We were incredibly happy, but gradually our priorities were changing.

We thrived so much, to the point of buying another home but this one was huge. It was almost 3,000 square feet. We built it from scratch. We chose the land and designed it to our liking; it was even in a highly desired place in the community. We now had one house there, one in Texas, and one in Puerto Rico. We were doing so good financially that we got good cars and even gave our kids everything they asked for. I was no longer cooking in the house as we ate out every day. I did not have enough time to cook for them because we spent most of our time working. When we were free from work, we liked to take the kids out of the house. In short, we lived like rich people. We had everything, but we lacked the most important thing, a relationship with God.

We attended church and even when our siblings opened their own, we helped them in ministry, but we did everything very systematic and purposefully. Our hearts were not aligned with Godly desires, but with those of worldly things. We had created self-sufficiency, especially me. Our lives began to be superficial, and we did not have intimacy with God. Although we never had problems in our marriage, we began to feel how our relationship cooled down; our priorities were different now, and the love of materialistic items took hold of our lives. This brought an opportunity for the enemy to attack me in my personal life. I had reached a point where my husband had not been able to fill the void I felt.

WE HAD IT ALL, BUT WE DIDN'T HAVE ANYTHING

I am not a person to talk much about money and prosperity, not because I am against these issues, but I understand that they are very controversial if they are not exposed in a correct and healthy way. There are many who fall into a dictatorial dynamic where they share a message of judgment and persecution for those who have the privilege of being wealthy. While some individuals are in need, others that are prosperous may cause many people to be frustrated with church services. The reasons may range from not having the money or capacity to be prosperous to not even being considered children of a King. Both extremes are bad but the balance and essence of what it really means to be children of a King and live kingdom lives are lost.

I am not an expert on this subject, but I can share my life experiences, which helped me better understand what it is to live a life through His kingdom. The life of the kingdom of God is simply based on modeling and reflecting the character of God and all that is around Him; it is the living experience of its essence. It is order, authority, justice, peace, but above all, the love that emanates from

Him and that all beings around Him imitate.

Materialistic belongings, money, professions, and even social or ministerial positions do not determine a life in His kingdom, but our attitudes toward everyone around us does. Humility is not determined by a social class; it is determined by the attitude of a grateful heart with God. I know people with less things who are prouder and more arrogant than many wealthy people. Just like I know people with a lot of money who are so humble that you would never think they are wealthy if you stumbled upon them on the street. It is a matter of attitude and how we shape the true character of Christ and the essence of the rule of the kingdom.

At that time, we were comfortable financially, but we experienced the most atrocious void of our lives, to the point where we became strangers to God. Our actions moved us away from our Father's house. We no longer sat down to eat at the King's table, yet we ate from the crumbs that were poured out to the pigs. All this because of our decision to move away from our home in the presence of God. We became puppets of a manipulative society that pressured us to act for convenience and not for necessity. It was convenient for us to be wealthy, but we needed God.

"Wealth and honor come from you; you are the ruler of all things. In your hands are strength and power to exalt and give strength to all. Now, our God, we give you thanks, and praise your glorious name."
(1 Chronicles 29: 12-13 NIV)

CHAPTER 26

Pornography

I started to get involved in the world of pornography and gradually I was sinking more into it. I began to open doors to the enemy and allowed him to subtly turn my life into a complete hell. The sexual fantasies we secretly imagined created a yoke that enslaved us. What we thought would join us more as a couple, in an unreal world, was moving us away from a reality that we now did not know how to handle.

We wanted countless times to leave our bad habits, but it was practically impossible. Our materialistic and superficial life fed more to our voids than our relationship with God. The more time we invested in the materialistic than in the spirit, we sank increasingly. I began to contemplate with the thoughts of making all the scripts come true that we imagined in secret. I struggled daily to want to do the right thing, but my thoughts tormented me constantly.

DON'T PLAY WITH FIRE, YOU WILL GET BURNED

Issues such as these are commonly a cause of controversy. We tend not to speak or expose them regularly because of fear, conservative ideologies inside and outside the church, or simply because we have wanted to normalize it in our society. The point is that this is almost never talked about; even resources regarding this are scarce, when looking for information about it. I would like to share my position on this, as I am a living example of the damage that pornography addiction can cause.

The consequences that I carried after my decisions were devastating, to the point where I almost lost my marriage. I even tried to take my life numerous times. The damages from the consequences of my actions did not end when we managed to restore our marriage, nor when I felt more emotionally stable. On the contrary, it is a struggle with which I fight daily. Yes, you read that well, I keep fighting with those thoughts and I decide to overcome them every day. The difference now is that my focus and my strength come from an inexhaustible source that I find in God.

Day by day, I decide to obey the laws and statutes designed for my benefit. When we think of laws, we automatically think of negatively enforced restrictions, especially when laws come from God. Many questions, criticize, and even become angry at not understanding or not being able to rationalize why a person can be obedient to a law created by a being that "cannot be seen with their own eyes."

My answer to this is that my decision to want to obey His laws daily has brought me the benefit of peace, joy, and real satisfaction in my loving relationship with myself and those around me. This is something I never found before I realized that His laws were created in love for my benefit. This has shown me that even though God is not seen, He is as real as my husband who sleeps next to me every night. The positive results I have received after giving my whole life, with my virtues and flaws, to God have been more than enough to believe 100% that He is real and that my life transformation is another example of the miracles He continues to do day by day. But let me explain a little more. Let me share with you some examples of experts on this subject, outside the religious or spiritual context, who share their positions from a clinical medical aspect in how this practice affects us as individuals personally and how we relate in this society. [2]Stanford University Doctor of Psychology Philip Zimbardo indicates that the constant consumption of pornography can present problems in "forming ties and creating intimacy in real life," because they have a misperception of sex and at times, it is difficult for a couple to get excited.

Dr. Albabeth Sárraga, a graduate of Carlos Albizu University in San Juan, Puerto Rico, shares the following, "Within the context of a couple, the construction of fidelity and trust is altered. For example, fidelity, because it is understood that sexual satisfaction can be achieved without the presence of the spouse. Confidence, since it opens up to the possibility that that satisfaction is in another. On the other hand, the issue of sexual satisfaction and expectation upsets the reality of the sexual life of the couple.

However, habituation to pornography can be perpetuated causing there to be no satisfaction in sexuality. As well as looking for other measures to seek sexual satisfaction."

In conclusion, I believe faithfully that pornography is a practice that does not bring anything positive to us personally or to society. On the contrary, it separates us from ourselves and those around us. Our decisions will always bring consequences, and I have stuck to continuing to make my decisions, even if sometimes it is difficult to exercise, but I obey and comply with divine laws, which do exist, believe or not. These laws were created out of love to help us reach our best version as living beings in this short and transitory life, not to take away from the reality of the problems and situations with which we will face. The purpose of these laws are to help us in the development of our character, which will also develop the beautiful dependency of an intimate relationship with God. This in turn will always bring rewards.

Dear reader, if you are one of those who just started seeing pornography, I advise you to stop. You are still in time to not immerse yourself in a life of darkness and dissatisfaction. On the contrary, if you have been struggling with this addiction for some time, I tell you that it is not too late; there is still hope. Turn over your weakness into His hands. I guarantee you that if you are faithful and obey Him, no matter how difficult you may find it to be, you will see a change and a transformation in your life. Do not be let down if you do it today and tomorrow you do not. God sees your heart and He will forgive you. The only thing He sees and asks from us is the willingness of our heart to want to change and our continued action to move away from our bad habits. It is Him who gives you the strength to overcome, but it is up to you to make the right decision every day. Do not give up. I know you can do it; you are not alone in this. There are many who fight day by day with our minds. The most beautiful thing about this walk is to know that even though many judge our condition, He will never do it. He is waiting for you with open arms to rest on His chest and feel His infinite love.

At the end of the book, I will leave you with the information of my great friend, Dr. Albabeth Sárraga, who can be a great resource to help you get out of this great battle you are in. It is wise to accept that we have a problem, but above everything, to make the decision to seek help from professionals who guide us in this process of transformation that God will make happen.

CHAPTER 27

Infidelity

On my way to work I met someone who made me feel different and awakened in me a desire to experience a life of adventure and lust. It all began by a simple conversation where I allowed that person to praise me. I remember that when I heard another man tell me pleasant words, it left a strong impression. Even though I was used to hearing my husband tell me these things every day, hearing them from another man provoked a completely innovative desire in me that I liked. Listening to my husband filled me with love but listening to them from another man awakened a feeling of passion for the forbidden. I knew it was wrong to let him talk to me like that, but I could not overcome temptation and it became an addiction. It was a relationship that we established through computer conversations and at lunch during work.

The most incredible thing was that the more I sank into darkness, the more the Holy Spirit touched Chapi and showed him that something was not going well with me. Three weeks after the beginning of this new relationship, Chapi confronted me. That day, he went to pick me up at work when I got off. On our way back to the house, I noticed that he turned away from our usual route and stopped at a public parking lot. I knew immediately what was going to happen; the Holy Spirit made me feel it. I became nervous and began to think of all the excuses I could say. When he turned the car off, he looked at me and started talking. I still remember that look he had as if it were yesterday; it was one full of pain and disappointment, something that instantly broke my soul. I could not continue to do this damage to him or my family. Embarrassed and frightened, I asked him why we had stopped there. He asked the question I was afraid of: "Are you with someone else?" I lowered my head and accepted my sin.

As expected, he was terribly upset. He began to hit the steering wheel while crying and yelled at me that our relationship was over. I was so scared because I had never seen him like that. I cried hopelessly, asking for forgiveness, swearing that I would end that relationship and not do it again; I felt so guilty and dirty. I do not know how we managed to get home in one piece because he drove in such a dangerous way that I thought at times we would die. We were able to get into the house without our kids knowing what was going on. We walked into our room and sat on the edge of the bed, and I cried out for the shame I felt. He went into the bathroom, then came out, took his keys again and left without telling me anything. I was left crying scared because I knew it had damaged our marriage.

Minutes later, one of my children knocked on the door because they were hungry. Listening to my children was even more painful. It was as if my spiritual eyes opened, and I could see everything clearly. I could see the lie in which I had been entangled in as if it had blinded me and I became accustomed to a dark and meaningless life. I could see the innocence of my children and the evil that enslaved me. I felt so miserable; it was an awakening to a reality that I had overlooked and disguised with my pleasure. I replied that I would come out in a moment. I asked them to wait a few more minutes while I showered. I tried to calm myself down and waited until the redness of my face went away from crying. When I went downstairs, I cooked them something fast and spent some time with them. I do not know how I achieved it; I was destroyed inside. It was time to sleep and while I was tucking them in, a feeling of fear flooded me. I thought it would be the last time I would be able to do this.

I went to bed hoping Chapi would return that night. I fell asleep while I was crying. In the early morning I got up because I suddenly felt my husband's head on my chest. While hugging me and crying, he told me that despite his pain, he would not allow the enemy to destroy his family. He had decided to forgive me and had been given the task of rebuilding our home, which I had destroyed. Even though I felt a slight relief from what I had heard, I did not know the worst was yet to come.

IT'S ALWAYS BETTER TO SPEAK THE TRUTH

The problem of lying is not only the action, but the consequences that it brings. Many times, we are afraid to confess our mistakes. Making the decision to remain silent is dangerous; this silence can destroy us from the inside out. It rots us to the point that we do not even smell our own nauseating smell. Our putrefaction not only pollutes us, but we damage everything we touch. Truth can prevent irreparable damage, while a lie that is not confessed condemns us a whole life.

"The Lord detests lying lips,
but he delights in people who are trustworthy."
(Proverbs 12: 22 NIV)

CHAPTER 28

My Life No Longer Had a Meaning

The days went by, and my life was crumbling; I had woken up from a horrible dream. Now I was facing a devastating nightmare that I lived awakened and one that devoured me and all my desires to live. Day by day, I struggled with my feelings of guilt. I hated to see myself in the mirror because I saw my dirt and all the trash I had accumulated up until then. I was blamed for everything that had happened. I felt like I was a bad daughter, bad sister, bad friend, bad mother, and especially a bad wife. All my destructive thoughts joined together, all those years for which I was battling with my character. I began to believe all the lies that the enemy told me daily. I was no longer walking with a straight posture; I was walking hunched over because of the weight I carried in my soul. I could not stop thinking how bad I was; how undeserving I was to be the mother of my children and the wife of a man who only loved me.

Loneliness seized me. I did not want to talk to anyone, nor tell them how I felt because I thought I deserved to feel like that. I began to analyze my life from when I was a child. I blamed myself for being born and for having felt rejected by my mom in my childhood and adolescence. Not being able to share more time with my dad; being a bad older sister, who physically and emotionally abused her little sister; being a bad younger sister since my older sister had a tough time tolerating me because of my personality....my whole life became one that made no sense.

When I looked in the mirror, I only saw a person who was always fighting, angry, full of hatred, full of pain, empty, a failure, lost, gross, ugly, and insensitive. I could still write more negative adjectives of how I felt and looked, but I would never finish the story. The enemy had used the right moment to detonate the bomb he had created and deposited in me for many years. At that time everything made sense...the best thing that could happen to all those around me was to no longer exist. The pain, suffering, disappointment, and discomfort that my life could make others feel would disappear if I did not exist.

I was immersed in a depression that only my husband and I knew about. I thought and planned every day and every night what the best way was to take my life. I tried to do it several times, but incredibly Chapi managed to avoid it all the time. Today I am amazed to see how God filled my husband with strength and love to help me get out of my darkness. I remember seeing him pray and cry on top of me while I was lying in a bed like a zombie. He used to play worship music for me to listen to while crying in bed. I do not know how my older children did not realize what their mom was going through. I can truly see God's hand in how He cared for and protected them. I used to pretend, in front of them and others, to be a person completely different from the one I hid in the depths of my darkness.

DEPRESSION AND SUICIDE

These two mental health disorders are real. Its effects are frightening and can be fatal if not attended to in time. If you are going through a situation like the one, I have experienced, I want you to know that you are not alone; that, although you see everything is dark, there is a small light at the end of the road waiting for you. It is time you decide to stop and leave the misery you find yourself in. It is time to take a deep breath and force yourself to walk towards that light. Not everything is lost, it is not the end; while you breathe, there will always be hope. It is not your time to die as you have not yet fulfilled your true purpose in this world. The time to rediscover yourself and see you, through the eyes of God, is now. In His presence you will find peace, in His presence you will discover your identity. God has come to visit you through this writing to let you know that He has always been at your side and has never left your side. He was just waiting for the moment for you to turn your eyes to Him.

I want you to do an exercise of faith at this moment and tell Jesus that you want Him to be the master of your life. At this time, I urge you to inhale His life, inhale His love, and exhale your fears and disappointments; those that have made you reach the point where you are at in these precise moments. Let go of all the destructive thinking that torments you; lay those thoughts in the hands of Him, who died on a cross and rose again on the third day, for your sake. For He promised to cleanse you and deliver you from your sins through His unmatched sacrifice. At this moment I declare that His beautiful presence will cover you and free you from everything and that you are healthy and free in the powerful name of Jesus. Amen.

I urge you to say this prayer with me, *"Lord Jesus, at this time I come to you in repentance, I confess my sins and ask you to forgive me. Clean me and purify me. Make me whatever you want. Teach me your ways and sign my name in the book of life. Today I accept you as my Lord or return to you. Never separate your Spirit from me, in the name of your beloved son Jesus. Amen."*

It is important that you also understand that it is of the utmost importance that you seek professional help from psychologists, pastors, counselors, or someone with clinical experience who can help you get out of the depression or negative mental condition you are in. God has given spiritual and clinical wisdom to specific individuals to help people like you and me overcome these situations that life presents to us. Seek help today!

"This is love: not that we loved God, but that he loved us and sent his Son as an atoning sacrifice for our sins." (1 John 4: 10 NIV)

CHAPTER 29

Love Covers a Multitude of Faults

In the midst of our pain, my husband heard the voice of God, who told him that it was time to return to Puerto Rico for a while so we could heal through what we had lived. God then removed all materials, our possessions, and gave us hope. I will never forget the words that Chapi told me after I shared my pain with him, knowing that we were going to lose everything we had achieved in North Carolina. He answered, "I prefer to live under a tree, without any of our belongings, but all together, rather than have it all and live in a mansion where I don't have my family."

Returning to the island was the best decision we could make. God used my apostles Luis and Doris Acevedo from our church, Ciudad de Refugio (City of Refuge), in the town of Morovis, which we attended before we left in 2010. They were the ones who helped us through the difficult process of restoration. My Apostle Doris, who I love and who I will be forever grateful to, is a psychologist in addition to her pastoral and apostolic calling. I remember that I used to have multiple sessions a month with her. These were exceedingly long sessions, which on many occasions, became moments of intercession and liberation for me.

It was a process of much pain and patience that we had to go through, not only me, but Chapi too. We became involved in church activities again. We served with our hearts, but with a lot of hard work, dying day by day to our humanity and our feelings.

We healed and were able to restore our marriage on that occasion. Many things became inconclusive in my personal life and in Chapi's life. Many things that I had not been able to overcome, such as my volatile character, with which I fought every day and my addiction to sex and pornography. I cannot question why God did not do it at that time; why He did not take his "magic wand" and free me from all my ties at that time. Now I understand that all my experiences only served so that I could have empathy with those who go through the same things I lived through, and we experienced in our marriage. At that time, I did not understand why He allowed me to experience all that, but now I know it is so that I can understand the pain and despair that you are going through.

We managed to prosper again in our finances and restore our marriage. Chapi and I entered a stage of our relationship where we experienced love that literally heals. We could not feel that we were far from each other because we were feeling a sense of fear and anxiety. We wanted to exchange words of intimacy that made us feel loved and secure. We slept hugging and cuddled all night and if we did not do so, we could not sleep. It was a time when love covered a multitude of faults. We experienced the power of love. We live in our own flesh as it says in:

TRUE LOVE *(1 Corinthians 13 NIV):*

"If I speak in the tongues of men or of angels, but do not have love, I am only a resounding gong or a clanging cymbal. If I have the gift of prophecy and can fathom all mysteries and all knowledge, and if I have a faith that can move mountains, but do not have love, I am nothing. If I give all I possess to the poor and give over my body to hardship that I may boast, but do not have love, I gain nothing.

Love is patient, love is kind. It does not envy, it does not boast, it is not proud. It does not dishonor others, it is not self-seeking, it is not easily angered, it keeps no record of wrongs. Love does not delight in evil but rejoices with the truth. It always protects, always trusts, always hopes, always perseveres.

Love never fails. But where there are prophecies, they will cease; where there are tongues, they will be stilled; where there is knowledge, it will pass away. For we know in part, and we prophesy in part, but when completeness comes, what is in part disappears. When I was a child, I talked like a child, I thought like a child, I reasoned like a child. When I became a man, I put the ways of childhood behind me. For now, we see only a

reflection as in a mirror; then we shall see face to face. Now I know in part; then I shall know fully, even as I am fully known.

And now these three remain: faith, hope and love. But the greatest of these is love."

CHAPTER 30

Second Infidelity

Our relationship was at the beginning of a deep restoration. The fires that would consume my sinful humanity and ties that alienated me from God had not completely ceased. That was just the beginning of becoming a new vessel; my Potter had not finished molding me yet. In early 2015, we heard the voice of God who told us that we should return to the United States. This time we felt no pain, no concern about leaving our island; although it may sound harsh, we felt that we no longer belonged there. Puerto Rico will always be the land where we were born and that we always love, but at that time we felt like outsiders. We knew our island was no longer our home...amazing, but true.

We returned to our home in Texas, which we had purchased in 2010. Everything was falling into place; Chapi found a decent job and I did too. Time passed on and again, we lost our focus on God and put our priorities on materialistic items and the desires of the flesh; my addiction to pornography was growing. First, we did it together almost every day and then we started doing it individually. Like all addictions, the feeling of pleasure is momentary and always leads you to seek more to satisfy that need. We began to have sexual fantasies where we saw ourselves having relationships with other people, especially with people of my same sex. Those desires made me think about what would happen if I could turn those fantasies into reality. We started evolving ourselves in that world and destroyed ourselves again, especially me, who had created an addiction with pornography and sex that I carried for years. While working, I met a man and again, I fell into temptation. My addiction had led me to the terrible decision to turn our fantasies into reality.

For the second time I was unfaithful, but this time I did not care if I lost my family or not. I had reached rock bottom. I experienced an even greater insensitivity in this type of sin this time around. I felt completely numb. I knew I was not in love with that other person, but the satisfaction of the momentary pleasure was greater than my willpower.

Also on this second occasion, the Holy Spirit showed Chapi what was going on. He confronted me again and embarrassed, I accepted my extramarital relationship. At that time, he told me that everything was over and that he was going to take away my children. That was what made me react. When I heard his words and saw his determination, I knew that I had lost everything, but this time it was true.

Although I did have sex with Chapi before marriage, our actions and ways of courting were quite healthy and innocent. However, what had awakened in me with this new person was something completely dirty that had come directly from hell itself. The most terrible thing about the matter is that I was aware of that. Every time I spoke to him, I was sincere about my feelings. I told him that the only reason I was with him was to satisfy my fleshly desires. I assured him that our relationship was not sentimental because I loved my husband and knew that Chapi was a much better man than he was. Amazing, but true.

I felt desperate and alone; I had no one to talk to and tell them through what I was living. I was embarrassed that, for the second time, I had committed the same sin and my family would be broken because of my lustful desires. God spoke to Chapi again and instructed him to stay next to me, even when he did not want to. On that occasion, God told him that it was going to be Him who would do the work in me.

SUNK IN A DEEP DARKNESS

Now I understand that the enemy had taken advantage of my bad decisions to start a war that he declared, where his mission was to kill us individually in a cruel and vulgar way. First, he started with me; he knew what area to attack me in. He knew my vulnerability and knew that at those times in our lives, God's presence had been removed from us by the life we had decided to live in in our intimacy as a couple. We had decided to live a life of darkness, of appearances before the world and before God. We were fighting with those desires and those fantasies. Many times, we wept and prayed together, but we came back and continued the same cycle. I know that God suffered more than us by seeing me and Chapi in the condition we were in, but He is a gentleman, a God who does not force us, nor does He impose anything on us that we cannot handle. It is not that God did not want to, it is that we, with our actions, already decided what we wanted. Even physics teaches us that where there is light, there is no darkness, and at those times, we lived in a cave where we understood something clearly at last from afar.

This is what a person who is completely tied to an addiction lives and experiences. He is aware that what he does is wrong, but the need to satisfy a desire is greater than anything else. I literally felt stuck and unable to get out of that vicious cycle in which I had entered.

"For our struggle is not against flesh and blood, but against the rulers, against the authorities, against the powers of this dark world and against the spiritual forces of evil in the heavenly realms. Therefore put on the full armor of God, so that when the day of evil comes, you may be able to stand your ground, and after you have done everything, to stand."
(Ephesians 6: 12-13 NIV)

CHAPTER 31

Our Plans Are Not God's Plans

A fter I left my job, Chapi was invited to a church we had seen in 2010 and wanted to visit. One day he told me, "We're going to visit it because it's Hispanic." He wanted to attend a church where they spoke Spanish. I accepted his invitation to please him, but I was doing it very defensively. I had made the decision to turn away from the ways of God because I felt I was a hypocrite and would fall back into my sin again. I had a posture of total rebellion.

I remember like it was today, that Sunday when we walked through the doors of my beloved church, Revive Worship Center, in the city of Killeen (which was then called Destiny). The shock I felt of the Holy Spirit was so powerful that the rebellious spirit I had upon me had to flee. I could not contain my tears when I heard the worship, and I could understand at that very moment that we had arrived home.

The months passed by, and God worked with us little by little. I remember that one night a call to the altar was made in my beloved church and I approached with

147

much conviction but was embarrassed because I came to God to ask for the same thing. This time my words were these, "Lord, please make my character more like yours." You might think that now I would have received an instant transformation, but it was not like that. In Puerto Rico there is a saying that says, "To the one who does not want broth, give him two cups." God gave me ten.

As soon as I told Him those words, the trials and situations in my daily life came one after the other, but this time I could see them in a different way. I saw them in a spiritual way. God began to work with my vision and how to see life through His eyes. I began to see people and life in another way; I began to love as Jesus loved. Perhaps, you will think it is corny or exaggerated, but that was how it was. That for me, will always be a miracle; a supernatural event in my life. I developed patience, empathy, understanding, and love for things, events, situations, especially love for people, as you could never imagine. I learned to be silent and quiet at times where I had previously given my opinion. Now God taught me to listen rather than speak. That is how it all started.

EMERGING FROM DARKNESS

Now I look back and imagine the pain and shame that Chapi went through, especially having to face all those thoughts in which society has deemed that infidelity for a man is worse than for a woman. I agree with this ideology to a certain extent; this destructive system is only to establish erroneous concepts and rules of what is right and wrong, therefore creating an imbalance of justice between a man and a woman. Unfortunately, a situation such as the one we experienced, is a living example of this.

We had to go through that process alone. No one knew what we were living out of fear of. We thought to ourselves, "What will they say?" We were afraid to be judged, marginalized, rejected, and in the end, we felt alone because of the deception that this society has created for this kind of situation, where women are the cause of infidelity, and man is the victim. Now I know that sin is sin, and we are measured under the same righteousness before the eyes of God. This is not that; if I am a woman and he is a man, it is a sinful condition that takes us away from God and destroys us as a person. The end of sin is the perdition that leads us to death and that, my sisters, and brothers, is the same result that both sexes will get. Glory to the Father for His infinite mercy and grace. Praise be His name because He always comes on time. It is in us to want to make the decision to listen and obey His voice. It is up to us to make the right decisions that will help us rise every time we do something wrong.

A relationship committed to God does not guarantee us a perfect life, but it does guarantee us a full life. A life full of light, which takes us away from that darkness of an empty and meaningless life.

Romans 6 (NIV) says:
"What shall we say, then? Shall we go on sinning so that grace may increase? By no means! We are those who have died to sin; how can we live in it any longer? Or don't you know that all of us who were baptized into Christ Jesus were baptized into his death? We were therefore buried with him through baptism into death in order that, just as Christ was raised from the dead through the glory of the Father, we too may live a new

life.

For if we have been united with him in a death like his, we will certainly also be united with him in a resurrection like his. For we know that our old self was crucified with him so that the body ruled by sin might be done away with, that we should no longer be slaves to sin— because anyone who has died has been set free from sin.

Now if we died with Christ, we believe that we will also live with him. For we know that since Christ was raised from the dead, he cannot die again; death no longer has mastery over him. The death he died, he died to sin once for all; but the life he lives, he lives to God.

In the same way, count yourselves dead to sin but alive to God in Christ Jesus. Therefore do not let sin reign in your mortal body so that you obey its evil desires. Do not offer any part of yourself to sin as an instrument of wickedness, but rather offer yourselves to God as those who have been brought from death to life; and offer every part of yourself to him as an instrument of righteousness. For sin shall no longer be your master because you are not under the law, but under grace. What then? Shall we sin because we are not under the law but under grace? By no means! Don't you know that when you offer yourselves to someone as obedient slaves, you are slaves of the one you obey— whether you are slaves to sin, which leads to death, or to obedience, which leads to righteousness? But thanks be to God that, though you used to be slaves to sin, you have come to obey from your heart the pattern of teaching that has now claimed your allegiance. You have been set free from sin and have become slaves to righteousness.

I am using an example from everyday life because of your human limitations. Just as you used to offer yourselves as slaves to impurity and to ever-increasing wickedness, so now offer yourselves as slaves to righteousness leading to holiness. When you were slaves to sin, you were free from the control of righteousness.

What benefit did you reap at that time from the things you are now ashamed of? Those things result in death! But now that you have been set free from sin and have become slaves of God, the benefit you reap leads to holiness, and the result is eternal life. For the wages of sin is death, but the gift of God is eternal life in Christ Jesus our Lord."

CHAPTER 32

My Crazy Love

Next, I would like to share the writing of a monologue in which God gave me the opportunity to minister at a women's conference that we have every year in my church. In this writing, God inspired me to write my testimony in a brief way:

Let me tell you about my crazy love. The One who rescued me. The One who made me emerge from darkness into the light.

I became a mother at the age of sixteen. I was unfaithful on two occasions.
I was addicted to sex and pornography for years. I
went into a deep depression for several months. I tried to take my life numerous times.
I battled with a character that destroyed me and those around me.
I was full of anger, hatred, envy, frustration, pain, loneliness, and I felt rejected.
All this, being inside the church.
But one day... I remember that one day I surrendered right here on this altar.
In the midst of my tiredness and despair of wanting to

change, I told God:

"God, I can no longer do this, I need you to intervene. I need you to do a miracle in my life because I do not think I can endure this double life that I portray any longer; even if I do not feel you, even if I cannot see you. Today I decide to surrender. Give me the opportunity to believe that I can be transformed.

Forgive me.

Clean my life and purify me. Free me.

Please make my character like yours. Fill me with your love.

Make a miracle in my life."

I remember that the moment I raised my hands and began to worship Him, I felt like chains were broken. I experienced, in a supernatural way, a peace that flooded my life. I literally felt light. Since that day I learned of a love that covers me and reminds me that nothing is impossible for those who believe in Him.

Since that day, I have discovered a crazy love that has made me see life from another perspective.

His love has made me a new person.

My transformation began when I received that love and decided to give it to others, even when I did not feel like it.

When I wanted them to forgive me, I forgave first. When I wanted them to love me, I loved first.

When I wanted mercy, I had mercy on others first. God's crazy and inexplicable love can be understood in some ways through the decisions we make daily.

Those decisions that make us servers and bearers of His immense love.

We discover that love when everything we want for us is first put into practice for others.

His love is reciprocal when we die to the "I" to let Him live through us.

God, I love our relationship, I love discovering You every day, but above all, I love this crazy love.

CONTINUOUS GROWTH

One of the most difficult things I have had to work with over the past few years is to try to convince those around me that I am a new person. It is normal that during this process, people closest to us will find it hard to believe or get used to our new version.

This is not because they do not like the transformation, but because it is difficult for everyone to act in a way, contrary to what we were used to before. Many times, the actions, or responses we receive after a conversation or simply a gesture we make will be enough to demonstrate our ability to love and act as Christ would. Also, not becoming defensive at the beginning of conversations, ensuring those around and close to us that we are in fact a changed person. It is all these trivial things that make this process one full of challenges.

What attracts people and convinces them is our testimony and how we act day by day. What impacts this is not just what we say, but how we say it. The love of God that we show in all that we do is the sweetness that attracts everything.

What is important is listening. Listen to others and

listen to God. When we listen, we learn and know the heart of who speaks. Finally, I still have a long way to walk, but now I am enjoying this path where I will always find stumbling stones. The biggest difference is that now I do not walk alone, but my Master accompanies me, who picks me up every time I fall and who will give me a lesson about each of those stones I will stumble upon.

I do not know if my calling is in arts, which I love to do so much, whether it is to teach, whether it is to preach, or just serve in any area where I am needed. I know that this will be one of many conversations we will have on this long walk. However, what I am sure of is that my heart will always be with the pencil and paper, where I translate my stories and my experiences about the love I found in God. A love that made me emerge from darkness into light.

BIBLIOGRAPHY

1 online consultation:
https://www.significados.com/los-4-tipos-de-amor-segun-l
os-griegos/

2 Taken from a column published in biobiochile.cl by
Javiera Iribarren

Contact information for my psychologist friend:
FB: Dr. Albabeth Sárraga
IG: @drasarraga

Made in the USA
Middletown, DE
21 September 2022

10391357R00094